HOW TO
CHANGE
YOUR
LIFE

HOW TO CHANGE YOUR LIFE

Five Steps
to Achieving
High Performance

Jake Humphrey

Damian Hughes

Cornerstone Press

1 3 5 7 9 10 8 6 4 2

Cornerstone Press
20 Vauxhall Bridge Road
London SW1V 2SA

Cornerstone Press is part of the Penguin Random House group of companies
whose addresses can be found at global.penguinrandomhouse.com

First published by Cornerstone Press in 2023

www.penguin.co.uk

A CIP catalogue record for this book is available from the British Library.

ISBN: 9781529903225 (hardback)
ISBN: 9781529903249 (trade paperback)

Typeset in 11.25 pt/16.7 pt Sabon LT Std by Jouve (UK), Milton Keynes
Printed and bound in Great Britain by Clays Ltd, Elcograf S.p.A.

The authorised representative in the EEA is Penguin Random House Ireland,
Morrison Chambers, 32 Nassau Street, Dublin D02 YH68

www.greenpenguin.co.uk

MIX
Paper | Supporting
responsible forestry
FSC® C018179

Penguin Random House is committed to a
sustainable future for our business, our readers
and our planet. This book is made from Forest
Stewardship Council® certified paper.

This book is dedicated to teachers across the world.
The unsung heroes who can change everything
for the next generation.

CONTENTS

CONTENTS

STEP V: ARRIVE

HOW TO CHANGE YOUR LIFE

We can always change.

THE JOURNEY AND THE MAP

Jake

I couldn't believe what I was hearing.

'This show is our chance to reward loyalty,' a senior colleague was saying down the phone. 'You haven't been loyal.' The result: I was being removed from the presenting team for the prestigious *Sports Personality of the Year* awards.

It was 2012, and I had just had the best year of my career. Earlier that summer I'd spent a month watching record after record fall at the London Olympics. I had spent weeks on a tour around Poland and Ukraine to report on Euro 2012. I had even been travelling the world to host my fourth season of the BBC's hugely popular Formula 1 coverage. Sport was amazing. My career was amazing. *Life* was amazing.

Except it didn't feel amazing then. My chat with that executive was only the most recent in a series of tough conversations. I had been told in no uncertain terms that things were about to change. It started with an awkward phone call with one of the bosses (Me: 'I appreciate all you've done for me and hope the door remains open.' Them: 'I'm afraid this is us closing the door' – followed by the line going dead). A little while later I was called into the office of a senior figure at *The One Show*, the BBC's flagship evening show. I had just finished hosting the show and had loved it, but as soon as we were off air the executive pulled me into their office to tell me I wouldn't be coming back after that week. It was the last time I hosted the show.

Eleven years of devotion to the job – from kids' TV to reporting on primetime sports and William and Kate's wedding – felt like it had gone up in smoke.

Why? Well, it had all started when my wife Harriet and I discovered we were going to have a baby. We were over the moon. But we had always known that having children was going to change the shape of my career. My role presenting Formula 1 for the BBC involved constant global travel and my wife was increasingly fed up with my long periods of absence. 'I didn't marry you only for you to move in with David Coulthard,' as she put it.

So I was looking for an excuse to travel less. And shortly later, a guardian angel swooped in to save me – taking the unexpected form of Arsenal legend Martin Keown. 'A friend of mine who works at BT has just asked if I know you,' Martin said to me one day when we were working together. 'Apparently she has an opportunity for you.'

A few weeks later I found myself in a meeting with his contact at BT. They had just spent over £700 million to acquire the rights to broadcast Premier League football. And they wanted me to front their new sports channel.

Following an extended bout of sometimes agonising soul-searching, the offer proved too good to resist. On paper, the job gave me everything I was looking for. Less travel. The rare chance to be a host of live football. And the once-in-a-career opportunity to launch a new TV channel from scratch.

On the other hand, I'd have to say goodbye to my beloved BBC – the place I'd worked since I was twenty-three years old, arriving with nothing but a few failed A-Levels and some not-entirely-relevant experience on local telly. The BBC had given me everything.

Fortunately, BT was nice enough to let me agree to carry out some work with my old employer. So I wouldn't be departing completely, right? Wrong. As I was now learning the hard way.

In many ways I understood the BBC response; I had chosen to walk away and had to suffer the consequences. But it was painful. In the weeks and months that followed, I started to worry that I'd made a catastrophic mistake. Early on, I went to a meeting to discuss the shape of the new channel BT was founding, BT Sport. The meeting was going to be with every single employee of the channel. Coming straight from the BBC, I was used to huge meetings with hundreds of employees listening to speeches from senior leaders. I turned up at BT's headquarters to find five other people in a boardroom. I'd left the oldest, most respected broadcaster in Britain – an operation with tens of thousands of staff – to join a team of about six. No studio, no production offices, no history – just lots of ambition and strong coffee.

If I was feeling on edge already, my anxiety only increased a few weeks later when I went to an awards show and a well-respected industry figure walked over and sat beside me. 'You must be shitting yourself,' they said.

'Why?' I replied innocently.

'Well, BT have paid almost a billion quid for football, and

it's all on your shoulders to deliver. Good luck!' They smiled warmly, patted me on the back, and wandered off into the crowd.

But within a few months, it was clear that BT Sport was on to something good. Those six staff members soon grew to ten, then twenty and beyond. And they were extraordinary: endlessly creative, hard-working and fun to be around. And their talent quickly delivered. Straight out of the gates, we filmed a huge TV advert on the Star Wars stage at Elstree Studios – which offered a glimpse of quite how ambitious this operation was going to be. Sure enough, within months, BT Sport had transformed commercial sports broadcasting. I was hosting FA Cup finals, huge Premier League matches, the Champions League. My unlikely guardian angel, Martin Keown, even came to join the channel.

It was the biggest leap I'd ever taken in my career. I'd experienced huge moments of doubt. Yet it had paid off.

That experience got me thinking. Soon, I realised that every big leap I had ever made had delivered something of value. Taking a leap by moving to London without a job to look for TV work. Taking a leap by putting my hat in the ring to present Formula 1. Taking a leap by founding my production company, the Whisper Group. And now taking a leap to leave the BBC.

What other leaps might I take – to improve my career, my hobbies, my relationships . . . my life?

Soon I found myself obsessing over the idea that knowing how – and when – to change holds the key to success in every sphere of my life. I came to live by the phrase 'hold your beliefs lightly'. Not becoming fixed was about the only thing I became fixed on.

And along the way, I realised something profound. That change shouldn't just be our reaction when things go wrong. Change should be what we do to ensure things go right.

The trouble is, change isn't something you're ever educated in. In fact, we find it naturally uncomfortable. In thirty-odd years, no one had ever shown me how high-performing people challenged themselves by seeking change – so they could realise their potential in sport, business, life.

I was learning a hard truth: that nobody ever teaches us how to change. We have to teach ourselves.

Over the years, that insight has guided me more than any other. And it's still guiding me today. After a decade at BT Sport, I'm now writing these words as a *former* employee. I left. Was I anxious? Of course I was. It was the first time since I left school I didn't have an actual job.

But over the years I had learned something obvious but powerful: that if you stop moving, you don't stand still. You end up going backwards.

I now know that if we want to succeed – *really* succeed – we need to learn to change. And if there's one man who has taught me that more than any other, it's my friend, co-host and mentor, Professor Damian Hughes.

Damian

I sat around a boardroom table watching my colleagues react to the bad news.

The problem was our margarine sales in Africa and the Middle East. Over the last quarter, they had dipped by 5 per cent.

I looked around the grand oak table to see how the meeting

would respond. Most of my colleagues, older and far more experienced than me, looked dejected – some outright bereft. But once they had got over the shock, they began to vigorously debate how best to reverse this alarming decline. Slowly, the momentum of the conversation started building towards potential solutions.

Soon, I noticed a pattern. Each of these charismatic and successful executives would take it in turns to express their dismay at the setback. Then they would suggest their own innovative plans to address the issue, drawing on all their creativity and hard-won market knowledge. As I watched each executive deliver their piece, a startling realisation started to creep over me: at some point, it was going to be my turn to speak.

And therein lay my problem. Because, as I worked through what I could possibly say, I experienced an epiphany. *I didn't give a shit.*

Not a single iota. There was not an atom of my being that thought this discussion had any significance whatsoever. I simply did not care about all that margarine.

'Damian, what are your thoughts?'

I shook myself and discovered a dozen pairs of eyes staring in my direction, politely waiting for my input.

'Well obviously, I'm completely devastated by the news.' I shook my head forlornly. 'But I do have some ideas on how we can arrest this situation . . .'

That night, I went home and looked at myself in the mirror with greater clarity than I'd had in years. The inner voice I'd forced to generate margarine-related business jargon hours previously was now vicious and unforgiving. I was ashamed of myself for behaving like a fraud (*You've got thirty more years of doing that, you idiot*). I was annoyed for allowing myself to be blinded by ambition without a sense of purpose (*You sold out. How much did it cost you to trade your dreams? A fancy job title and a final salary pension?*). Most of all, I was confused about how on earth I had found myself here.

Having grown up in a boxing club, I had long appreciated environments that placed a premium on community – and particularly cultures where everyone felt valued and able to perform at their best. Initially, this had led me to a career that might loosely be described as coaching: helping leaders in many different industries and worlds to create cultures where people could thrive.

In time, that led to a focus on business cultures – and in turn a job in the corporate world. I had no prior experience of this universe and had slowly, imperceptibly, been seduced by the comforts it offered. The regular salary. The company car. The business-class flights. They had impressed me – and then blinded me. Without realising it, I had come to believe that climbing the corporate ladder represented true success.

Until that day in the boardroom. That afternoon, I finally slammed up against the famous 'Peter principle': the moment you reach your first level of incompetence, I knew I'd taken a wrong turn. I now understood that old joke about how meetings are 'where minutes are taken but hours are wasted'. I was trapped in endless catch-ups about how other people could do the very kind of work that I loved doing.

The sleepless night that followed was the moment I resolved to change things.

What followed was a lot of honest – and, at times, uncomfortable – self-reflection. I mentally resigned from my role before I worked up the courage to follow through properly a few weeks later. In that time, I went looking for a new path. I wanted a new role, a new career – a new life.

But it would take me a little while to know where to go. Before I could move, I needed to understand where the changes to come would take me. I needed to know where I was going.

DRAWING THE MAP

It would take us some time, but eventually we'd both find our way. These days, we your authors spend most of our time meeting remarkable people for the *High Performance* podcast, and trying to delve into what they can teach us. Along the way, we've stumbled upon some answers to the big question we both asked: *How do people change their lives?*

The answers we've found are surprisingly simple. On the pod, we've become fond of describing high performance as a race car. It looks alarmingly complicated. In truth, it's just a collection of simple parts put together well. An efficient engine. A well-designed chassis. Four slick wheels. If you get these basic components right, your car will soon be zooming along the track.

In our last book, *High Performance*, we introduced the parts that make up this car. We explored the mental habits high performers use to take responsibility for their situation; the non-negotiable behaviours they use to perform under pressure; the methods they use to lead others.

But our focus was on how to build the car, not where to take it. We didn't attempt to detail the hairpin bends, the chicanes, or the straight lines where you could really put your foot down. We didn't tell you the best moment to start on your journey, or what to do if you get stuck, or how to tell if you're close to your end goal.

So that's where this book comes in. It will show you exactly how to get from where you are to where you want to be. It's the A–Z in the glove compartment of your high-performance vehicle.

We've started from a simple assumption: that everybody wants to change something about their lives, however small. It might just be learning to excel in a side hobby (indeed, one of our favourite correspondents told us she's been using our podcast to improve her macramé skills). It might be getting a new job or improving your relationships. It might be as drastic as rebuilding your whole life from scratch.

But in every case, we hope this book offers a toolkit to help you fire up the engines and start going where you want to. High performance is a journey. This book is your roadmap.

FIVE STEPS TO CHANGE YOUR LIFE

This all raises an obvious question. *Surely it's not possible for one book to offer a guidebook to anyone who wants to change – whatever their situation?* After all, everyone's situation is different. Besides, it's pretty much impossible to predict where any individual's life will go next. As the World Cup-winning rugby coach Sir Clive Woodward put it: 'Success doesn't happen in straight lines.'

'Success doesn't happen in straight lines.' Sir Clive Woodward

And you'd be right: there is no one-size-fits-all guide to changing your life. Every situation is different.

But then, as the writer Mark Twain said: 'History never repeats itself, but it does often rhyme.'

What on earth was he talking about? To answer that, we've created a simple quiz. Read the following passage about one of our interviewees closely because there'll be a test at the end:

X was stuck in rut. They weren't performing as well as they wanted to in their work, and it was bringing down their mood. After a while, they started to wonder: What if I made a huge, dramatic change? Eventually, they couldn't bear it any more. They took a terrifying, bold leap into the unknown. Predictably enough, it went terribly. They faced setback after setback, and even started to regret taking the plunge. But with time, they started to see some signs that their new life was more rewarding than their old – and that they were learning skills they'd never imagined they could. Ultimately, they found themselves in a wholly new situation – one that was so rewarding they wanted to share what they'd learned with everyone they knew.

Question 1 for 1,000 marks: Who is this passage about?

a. **Ben Francis:** the founder of the billion-pound sportswear company Gymshark stepped down as CEO because he didn't have the requisite experience – only to triumphantly return years later after he had spent half a decade developing the right skill set.

b. **Alex Scott:** the England footballer who was told by everyone she knew that she definitely shouldn't move to the US women's soccer league – only to unexpectedly use what she learned in Boston, Massachusetts, as a springboard to launch a record-breaking career in international football.

c. **Tyson Fury:** the world-beating boxer who, after suffering debilitating depression and falling into terrible form, came back from three years of inactivity to reclaim his position as world heavyweight champion.

You're a smart bunch, so you've probably realised this is a trick question. The truth is, this story describes *all* of the high performers above. They each dreamed of a new life: returning as CEO, becoming an England footballer, regaining world champion status. They each fought through the obstacles: a lack of experience, naysaying colleagues, mental illness. And they each became modern-day legends: *the* Ben Francis, *the* Alex Scott, *the* Tyson Fury.

And it wasn't just those three. Over the last few years, we have come to realise that almost all our high performers' stories – from rugby players to teenage entrepreneurs to political strategists – followed this trajectory. The changes were different. But the journeys were remarkably similar.

We weren't the first people to notice, either. In 1949, the American literature professor Joseph Campbell published a book called *The Hero with a Thousand Faces*.[1] Campbell noticed that an inordinate number of works of literature tell the same story. They feature an ordinary-seeming individual from a modest background who is 'called to action'. The young hero travels from his humdrum little world to a 'region of supernatural wonder' and encounters fabulous forces, has various helpers and wins a great victory. He then returns to 'bestow boons' on his home community. Think of Luke

Skywalker in Star Wars. Or Bilbo Baggins in *The Hobbit*. Or Katniss Everdeen in *The Hunger Games*. Campbell called this story the 'monomyth'.

According to Nancy Duarte,[2] one of the world's foremost communication experts, this is the basic story that underpins the way humans make sense of any change process. Anyone who is seeking to get from any here to any there will have to go through the following steps:

1. **Dream.** You start to imagine a future that is better than your current reality. This dream needs to be something that excites and enthuses you.
2. **Leap.** You commit to a particular set of actions and behaviours, taking the first jump towards your dream life.
3. **Fight.** You experience some difficulty and maybe some pain. These obstacles are a sign you are on the right track and are part of the journey, rather than something to be avoided.
4. **Climb.** You start spotting the 'seeds of progress' – some small wins that are taking you to the end goal.
5. **Arrive.** You reach your destination – but a destination is not an end point. Change is a continual process, so you now start all over and go back to Step I.

Inspired by Nancy Duarte and Joseph Campbell, Ben Francis and Alex Scott, Bilbo Baggins and Katniss Everdeen, we have organised our book around these five steps. First, we explain how to Dream of a new life – and take a Leap into it. We'll explore how to work out what it is about your life that you actually want to change (it's rarely quite what you think). And we'll examine how to lay the ground for your change journey – focusing on how the environments we place ourselves in determine how successful our jump into the unknown will be.

Next, we examine the Fight and Climb stages. We'll examine the three biggest obstacles people encounter on the road to change – and how to reframe the setbacks that do happen so they don't blow you completely off track. And we'll reveal how to sustain yourself on the long journey to success, by turning one-off behaviours into reliable systems that will take you to the summit.

Finally, we'll examine what to do when you Arrive. This moment can be euphoric – but it can also be dangerous. We'll show you how to avoid complacency when you've achieved what you set out to, and how to find your next journey – one that will turn a single change into a continual process of improvement.

Every change is different. But every change follows the same path – a path that millions of people have navigated before. You aren't the first person to change your life, and you won't be the last.

THE LONG ROAD TO A DIFFERENT 'YOU'

A frankly alarming number of years have passed since those two, all-important afternoons – when Jake quit the BBC and Damian fabricated some provocative opinions on margarine. In the years since, our lives have taken us in vastly different directions – but both ended with *High Performance*. Without realising it, we were reading the same map – and walking the same path.

It hasn't always been easy. Damian doesn't miss that boardroom; Jake certainly doesn't hope to be dismissed from any more BBC positions. But the journey did teach us both an important lesson: that however stuck you are, however long things have been this way, however deflated you might feel, *we can always change.*

Jake learned it when he left the BBC. Damian learned it when he told his boss that he had been lying a little bit about his interest in vegetable spreads. And we're not alone. If there's one thing we've discovered in the course of the hundreds of hours of interviews for our podcast, it's that everybody – from billionaire founders to world-leading coaches to record-shattering athletes – has had moments like this.

We all have times when things just feel wrong. We all have moments when we're stuck in a rut. We all have moments when life calls on us to make a change.

The key to high performance is how we respond.

Ready? Then let's begin.

Dream

Every change starts with a dream.

To dream of a new life, you must first understand this one.

WHAT'S YOUR PROBLEM?

Forty bright-eyed students crowded around two large tables, each piled high with an array of objects: a bunch of grapes, a brass horn, and a glass prism. The instructions from their teachers were simple: pick up a few of the items on the table, head back towards your easels, and then draw a still life.

These twenty-something students were a talented bunch. This was the prestigious School of the Art Institute of Chicago, one of America's most renowned colleges for the fine arts. And these were fourth year students, well on their way to becoming some of the United States' brightest young artists. As the students bustled around their table, two men stood in the background making notes on how they behaved – and keeping a close eye on what they drew.

This case study might sound like any old final-year examination. In fact, it was more special than that. Because the instructor who invited them to create their still life was not an art professor, but one of the world's most renowned psychologists. And he was not interested in the quality of the art itself. He was interested in something even grander: the nature of human creativity.

It was the 1960s, and the man leading the examination, Mihaly Csikszentmihalyi, had already began his famous research on the 'flow state' – that rare sensation when creative effort feels easy and carefree.[1] This new project, designed in partnership with his colleague Jacob Getzels of the University of Chicago, was an attempt to work out how one might induce it.[2]

Csikszentmihalyi was less interested in the time spent drawing – and more intrigued by the time spent selecting objects from the tables. The approaches the artists took were remarkably diverse. As Daniel Pink later wrote: 'Some examined relatively few objects, outlined their idea swiftly, and moved quickly to draw their still life. Others took their time. They handled more objects, turned them this way and that, re-arranged them several times, and needed much longer to complete the drawing.'[3]

As Csikszentmihalyi saw it, those who chose quickly were immediately trying to *solve* a specific problem, namely: *How can I produce a good drawing?*

Those who took their time and tried several different arrangements were actively trying to *find* a problem to solve: *What would be a fascinating challenge to draw?*

Csikszentmihalyi was intrigued by which approach led to better-quality art. So at the end of the drawing session, he arranged a showing of the final drawings, for which he had recruited a panel of art experts to assess and judge the work.

The experts were unanimous: the students who produced the

best work were not those who rushed headlong into drawing. Nor were they the ones who were most technically competent. They were the ones who took their time at the table, reflecting deeply on what lay before them. The problem-finders.

This moment marked the beginning of a research project that would continue for decades. Csikszentmihalyi and Getzels tracked down the same artists ten years later and discovered that those who were still producing art had one thing in common: they were almost exclusively the problem-finders identified a decade earlier. In contrast, most of the problem-solving group had given up on their artistic ambitions. Another decade on, a further follow-up found the artists who were most prone to problem-finding continued to achieve greater success than their more solutions-minded classmates.

Csikszentmihalyi and Getzels' conclusion was succinct: 'The quality of the problem that is found is a forerunner of the quality of the solution that is attained.'[4]

This idea has been a consistent theme throughout our own interviews with high performers. We have consistently found that the first step to changing your life is to come up with a new vision of what could be – to dream of another way of being. Every change starts with a dream. But the best dreamers are not the ones who rush headlong into imagining another life without thinking. They are the ones who take their time to think, slowly and critically, about the problems they face right now. The ones who ask, *What is actually making me unhappy? What is preventing me from achieving my goals?* The problem-finders.

Problem-finding is not just *as* important as problem-solving; it is arguably *more* important. To dream of a new life, you must first understand this one.

EXPLORE YOUR PROBLEM

Lewis Morgan seemed nervous.

We were backstage at the Town Hall in Birmingham, the home city of the charismatic co-founder of British sports brand Gymshark who is today the chairman of the UK's fastest growing brand, AYBL. But being close to the streets he'd grown up on wasn't offering Morgan much solace. As we waited to step out before an enthusiastic crowd, Morgan turned to us and candidly admitted: 'I'm not sure what I've got to talk about; I'm winging it.'

But as soon as he stepped out on stage, Morgan's nerves seemed to evaporate. He looked completely in his element. A natural talker, his hands moved like a conductor leading an orchestra. He didn't seem to be winging it at all.

Morgan was about to offer us one of the most powerful insights into problem-finding that we had ever encountered. His experience with Gymshark had been remarkable. Having co-founded the sportswear company in 2012 at the age of twenty, he had grown it into a £400 million business. By his thirtieth birthday, he was being hailed as one of the most successful businesspeople of his generation. And that success, it seemed to us, wasn't just about hard work, talent, or even luck. It was about how he approached problems.

When we asked Morgan about the secret of his success, he said the ability to approach a situation without any preconceptions was key. 'It was our inquisitiveness to keep diving down rabbit holes that led us to places that eventually made money,' he told us of his early days working with his co-founder, Ben

Francis. 'I'm probably one of the most uneducated people but when I see a good idea, I just explore it.'

'When I see a good idea,
I just explore it.' Lewis Morgan

Easy enough to say, we thought. But how would he prove it? We tested him out by asking how he would take £100 and use it to make multiples more. Most people would probably say they'd invest it in stocks or maybe loan it to someone and charge interest. Not so Morgan. 'I'd just buy loads of different things, like golf gloves, old furniture, and I'd start by selling 'em on,' he said. 'How many people give away a couch every single day for free because they can't be arsed to get rid of it? I'll take that and I'll bung it on for twenty quid.'

Morgan's answer wasn't just compellingly creative. It also hinted at the first way we can find our real problems. All too many of us approach the issues we encounter – how to change £100 into £1,000, how to change our career, how to change our lives – with a preordained set of solutions. We see the world through a particular lens. And we never take it off.

These preconceptions colour our thinking in ways we barely realise. Consider a paper from Stanford University. Scientists recruited some volunteers who divided into two groups: the 'tappers' and the 'listeners'. Tappers received a list of twenty-five well-known songs, such as 'Happy Birthday' and 'Yankee Doodle Dandy'; they were asked to pick a song and tap out the rhythm to the listener. The listener's job was simply to guess the song.

Before they began, each tapper was asked a question: How many songs would the listeners manage to guess? They predicted that it would be over 50 per cent.[5]

The reality was startlingly different. Of the 120 songs that were tapped out, listeners guessed only 2.5 per cent of the songs correctly. A grand total of three songs.[6] The lesson – explained in Professors Chip Heath and Dan Heath's excellent book *Made to Stick* – is that our preconceptions dramatically change how we see the world. When you tap a tune yourself, you know what to expect – and so hear the song naturally. When someone else taps it, you hear nothing of the sort, just a bunch of disconnected noises. As the Heath brothers summarise it: 'Once we know something, we find it hard to imagine what it was like not to know it.'[7]

What does this mean for the way we approach problem-finding? Well, when we embark on a change journey, it is all too easy to make assumptions about the issue before us. You don't like your job and assume that the problem is that you haven't been promoted in two years. You don't like your home life and assume that the problem is that you've not been getting along with your partner. You don't like your hobby and assume that the problem is that your skills aren't improving quickly enough. In every case, you might be right – but without further investigation you'll never know.

But like Morgan found, there is a simple way around these mental blocks. The trick is to adopt an inquisitive mindset – and ask yourself, *Is there another way to look at this problem? Is there an obstacle here I'm not seeing?* Or, as Morgan put it, 'just explore it'.

Here, it can be helpful to draw upon the insights of your friends and peers. Through our conversation with Morgan, he often referred to his early conversations with Ben – and how they helped him see the problems his fledgling business encountered afresh. It's an insight we can all learn from. When you speak to others, you might discover that the issue isn't the promotion, but your mindset at work. That the issue isn't your partner, but rather your antagonistic approach to your daily interactions. That the problem isn't the speed of your learning, but the hobby you've chosen in the first place.

Other people's perspectives help us see through our preconceptions and explore our problems with greater clarity. The supermodel, activist and entrepreneur Lily Cole was the most skilled interviewee at making this leap. When we sat with her and posed questions about her career and the lessons she had acquired, she would always end her answers by asking: 'What about you? What do you think? What have you learned?'

Whenever you feel like you don't understand the issue before you, ask the people around you what they see – their answers might surprise you.

REFRAME YOUR PROBLEM

Once you have started to explore your problems, it becomes easier to see them for what they really are. But you're still not a fully qualified problem-finder, not yet. Because exploring the problem isn't the same as truly understanding it.

To explain what we mean, join us for a brief thought experiment suggested by the wonderfully named Thomas Wedell-Wedellsborg, a world expert on problem-solving. 'Picture the scene: you are the owner of an office building and your tenants keep complaining about the lift. It's old and slow and keeps breaking down; in fact, it's so unreliable that your tenants keep threatening to move out if you can't solve the problem. What do you do?

'When asked, most people quickly identify some solutions: replace the lift, install a stronger motor, or perhaps upgrade the algorithm that runs the lift,' Wedell-Wedellsborg writes.

But these answers are 'plain boring'. They are all 'falling into the solution space: a cluster of solutions that share assumptions about what the problem is'. In this instance, this cluster concludes that the problem is the lift: it is too slow.

Is there an alternative solution? Yes, says Wedell-Wedellsborg: and it's devilishly simple. Put up mirrors next to the lift. 'This simple measure has proved wonderfully effective in reducing complaints,' he writes, 'because people tend to lose track of time when given something utterly fascinating to look at – namely, themselves.'[8]

This isn't a solution to the problem as originally identified. The lift is not magically faster, nor more reliable. Instead, we have reframed what the problem actually *is*.

This is the second step in effective problem-finding. Once you have explored your problem, you might want to reframe it – and look at it from a different angle.

Easier said than done, you might think. How can we learn to habitually reframe our problems – and in turn find better solutions? One answer comes from Steve Clarke, who we once interviewed in front of 2,000 *High Performance* listeners in Edinburgh. The Scotland national football team coach told us that he had come into the role convinced that he knew the solutions his team needed. The issue, he thought, was about the style of play. With a new strategy, everything would change.

It was only after some chastening defeats early in his leadership that he took a long walk and recognised that he was stuck – because the problem wasn't the playing style, it was the mindset. Scotland just thought of themselves as habitual losers, he told us. 'Scotland has always had great players but I had underestimated how psychologically deep-rooted this mindset was,' Clarke told us. 'I needed to find a way to change this losing mentality where we just turn up, we get beat, we get knocked out and the manager gets sacked.'

And so he came up with a radical new approach. Now he asked himself a different question. Instead of asking, *What formation will lead to success?*, he set himself an alternative challenge, asking, *What mindset will lead to success?* With this reframing device, his focus moved from players' physical behaviour on the pitch to their mental behaviour off it. 'We stopped playing with a fear of failure and starting playing with an expectation of success,' he told us. Clarke's approach led Scotland to their first international tournament in twenty-two years.

 'We stopped playing with a fear of failure and started playing with an expectation of success.' Steve Clarke

This is a method anyone can draw upon. The trick is simply to pause and ask yourself some basic questions. *What assumptions am I making about the problem before me? Is there a different way to think about the challenge I face? Is there a different question I might be asking myself?*

When we were at school, one of the most common pieces of teacherly advice was to make sure you read the question on the exam paper before you start writing your answer. In our busy lives, there is often a similar desire to rush straight into problem-solving mode.

We assume we know what the question is without checking. But the consequence is often the same: the wrong answer.

CLARIFY YOUR PROBLEM

As we waited to meet Alastair Campbell for his *High Performance* interview, your two authors admitted to one another that they felt a little nervous.

We are both fans of Malcolm Tucker, the 'attack dog' spin doctor in the comedy drama *The Thick of It* famous for haranguing unfortunate journalists with his strident style of questioning and creatively profane insults. Tucker was at least partly based on Campbell, the former prime minister Tony Blair's spokesman, press secretary and director of communications, and one of the most influential – and controversial – figures in recent British political history. One of our favourite insults from Tucker's back catalogue is: 'The guy is so dense that light bends around him.' We were steeling ourselves for a similarly pithy takedown.

So imagine our surprise when Campbell proved to be the personification of charm. He cracked jokes, asked us about our families and shared his contagious love of Burnley Football Club. Above all, he talked with enormous candidness and power about his struggles with mental illness.

These struggles have haunted Campbell for decades. His

family history is dotted with mental ill health. One brother, he once told a journalist, lost both of his legs – 'one for the booze and one for the fags', before dying at the age of sixty-two. Another 'loved people and loved life' but suffered from severe schizophrenia and died at the same age.[9] Campbell too has had severe depression since he was young. A recovering alcoholic, he suffered his first major psychotic episode in 1986 in the midst of a political party conference. Today, Campbell has long since kicked the booze – but mental illness remains a recurrent feature of his life. His book *Living Better* has the striking opening line: 'On a dark Sunday night last winter, I almost killed myself.'[10]

Campbell does not view his mental illness as something that will ever be permanently 'cured' – rather it is a part of his life that he must learn to manage. And that's how he led us to an unusual – but profound – observation about how to clarify to ourselves the biggest problems that we face.

In 2019, while filming a documentary on depression, Campbell met a Canadian geneticist counsellor, Jehannine Austin, to talk about his family history of mental illness.[11] Dr Austin emphasised that, whatever the nature of your mental health, you can learn to understand it – and have some agency over how you manage it. Her analogy is what she calls a 'mental illness jar', which is filled with all the factors that affect your wellbeing, both in and out of your control.

Your basic biological make-up is the bottom layer. 'Down at the bottom of the jar is the sediment – your genes,' Campbell recalls her saying. In his case, this meant an inherited predisposition to mental ill health. But that's not all that goes into the jar. 'The rest of your jar is your life,' Campbell went on, including job issues, relationship problems, financial worries and personal loss. Some people are unfortunate enough to be born with more sediment in the jar than others – but it could fill up for anyone. And when our jar is overflowing, our mental health suffers. 'When the jam jar gets full, it means you can't cope,' Campbell says. 'The lid explodes and your life explodes and you're ill.'[12]

But the joy of the jam jar is that you don't just need to fill it up with problems. You can fill it up with the things you love – whatever it is that will help you feel happier and live better.

Campbell credits the jam jar with helping him clarify the real issues he faced – and the real solutions. Once, during a bout of depression, 'I got up in the middle of the night and drew my own jam jar,' he told us. He realised that he could fill it with the things that brought him joy. 'The first thing is FFF: Fiona [his wife], family, friends. If my key relationships are strong, if my kids are reasonably happy, if Fiona and I are getting along, if I've got a small number of close friends that I totally trust, that's not a bad start.' And he could choose to fill up the next layer with things that brought him meaning: 'which means work, but it also means changing the world'.

Above that came the more quotidian – but no less important – sources of happiness: 'sleep, diet, exercise, which I never used to take seriously and now I do.' And above that are the smaller, everyday pleasures: Burnley FC, bagpipes, trees, Elvis, Jacques Brel, Abba, his bike, his dog. 'These are the things that matter to me,' Campbell laughed as he riffed through his list. Finding these little joyous things – and putting them into your jam jar – holds the key to a well-adjusted life.

What does a jam jar have to do with problem-finding, you might, understandably, be asking? Well, it hints at how we can move from exploring and reframing our problems to truly understanding them.

Like Campbell, we all need a method to clarify the bewildering and complex problems we face in our lives. One of the reasons we struggle to change is that the problems we face are too complicated to process. We don't truly 'get' our issues because they are overwhelming. You know you're unhappy about some aspect of your relationship, but it's hard to work out *what*. You know you're dissatisfied with the career you've chosen, but you can't figure out *why*.

Campbell's method hints at the solution – and not just in the context of mental health. The simple act of actively visualising what is causing our distress – and writing it down – transforms our ability to process it. This is an idea with a strong grounding in science: studies have shown, for example, that writing about a traumatic experience for fifteen minutes a day can lead to improved health outcomes months afterwards.[13] In another, participants 'who wrote about the most stressful event of their lives experienced better health evaluations related to their illness.'[14]

One need not be battling with great trauma to undertake this process. You can apply it to your own daily existence. What is in your jam jar – and how close is it to being full? Now look more closely: what are the biggest objects – and are they bringing you joy or not? If you were to take out one big object and replace it, what would it be? And how does that help you clarify the problem you face? Is the problem with your job, your relationships, or your hobby really the one you're fixating on – or is it something else entirely?

According to Campbell, this method is one of the simplest and most powerful mindset shifts you can make – one that allows us to simplify our problems into a form we can properly understand.

It's an unexpectedly revolutionary method, he says. 'Before I met this woman in Canada, if you had said to me, how do you cope with depression? I'd have said I take medication every day,' says Campbell. 'I still take medication, but if you now say to me, how do you deal with depression? I'll say, 'Oh, I've got me jam jar.'[15]

PITSTOP - JAM JAR

The best way to see a problem clearly is to write it down. That's what the jam jar below is for. Take a moment to fill it up with what matters the most to you right now. Then ask yourself, *What would a happier jam jar look like? Is there a way to make it more meaningful and fulfilling? And what does that tell you about the problems you face?*

LESSON SUMMARY

What is the one thing in your life that's bringing you down – and what can you do to change it?

- We think that change is all about finding solutions. But we're wrong. The first step to changing yourself is identifying the issue itself – moving from problem-*solving* to problem-*finding*.
- The problem-finder's toolkit contains three key methods. First, explore your problem. Look at your life and ask: *What is the biggest issue I face?* Ask the people around you: *How do they see your problems, and what can you learn from them?*
- Second, reframe your problem. Our preconceptions often prevent us from seeing the problems before us clearly. But you can eradicate these preconceptions with relative ease. Ask yourself: *What assumptions am I making about the problem before me? Is there another way to view it?*
- Third, clarify your problem. The simple act of writing your issues down helps you distill them into a form you can understand. Grab a pen and paper and write down the biggest issues you want to solve. *What is bringing you down the most – and what would a better life look like?*

If you can find happiness, you might just find health too.

A BETTER 'YOU'

Britain's favourite doctor was telling us about a group of very happy nuns.

These nuns were ideal experimental subjects, Rangan Chatterjee told us in his calm, melodic voice, because everything about their lives was regulated by the monastery. They all had the same lifestyle, diet, movement and sleep. And this, a group of psychologists had noticed, represented a research opportunity.

'They followed these nuns their entire life,' Dr Chatterjee said, nodding effusively.[1] By doing so, they were able to assess what really made the difference in how long they lived. The answer? 'The happier nuns were significantly healthier and they lived for longer.' Being happy improved their health outcomes across the board.

That wasn't the only insight into happiness the doctor had in store for us. 'Another study took people into a lab and measured their happiness before putting the rhinovirus up their nostrils,' he said, his voice wavering with excitement.

Everyone in the study was exposed to the virus. The question was: *Who would get sick?* Once again, the key determining factor was not their physical condition – but their mood. 'What they found was that three times the number of people got sick in the "not so positive mood" category,' he said. 'You could determine who is more likely to get sick based upon their happiness.'[2]

Chatterjee was not just telling us about this research because it was interesting, although it certainly was. He said it was the key to an insight that had transformed his life. By the time he came on our podcast, Chatterjee had spent twenty years working as a doctor, first as an immunologist in hospitals up and down the country. But the more he specialised in people's physical health, the more he realised it was impossible to understand it without investigating their mental health. 'This link is very underappreciated, across society, but also within the medical profession,' he said in one interview.[3]

This epiphany had become a fascination of Chatterjee's. By the time we met him near his Cheshire home for the podcast interview, the links between happiness and health were an all-consuming obsession. He was on a mission to transform how his fellow doctors – and the world in general – thought about mental illness. In fact, he'd just written a book about it: *Happy Mind, Happy Life*.[4]

The more important Chatterjee realised happiness was, he told us, the more intrigued he became with another simple question. *Is our happiness something that we have any control over – and if so, how do we change it?* The answer led him to an ancient Japanese concept – one that your authors too would soon become obsessed with. It goes by the name of *Ikigai*.

There is no direct English translation for *ikigai*. A compound of the word *iki*, which means life, and the word *gai*, which describes value or worth, it's a term that means little more than living well. Popularised by the excellent book *Ikigai: The Japanese Secret to a Long and Happy Life* and explained to us in a podcast interview with its quietly spoken but endlessly engaging co-author Héctor García, there is a growing body of evidence that people with good *ikigai* aren't just happier – they actually have longer lives. If you can find happiness, you might just find health too.

So what is this enigmatic *ikigai*? 'It's about alignment,' Chatterjee told us. 'If you can figure out what your core values are and how you live each day in accordance with those values, you get meaning and purpose as a by-product.' But how? Well, in their book, García and Miralles encourage us to find out by asking a few related questions (in their case four, though we find it helpful to simplify them down to three).

1. *What are you good at?*
2. *What do you love?*
3. *What does the world need?*[5]

At the intersection of your three answers lies your *ikigai*. And this method hints at how to turn the problems we identified in the previous lesson into a practical vision of a new life. If you can dream of a life at the point where these three answers meet, you won't just feel happier; you might just live longer too.

PITSTOP - *IKIGAI* FINDER

Héctor García and Francesc Miralles conceptualise *ikigai* as a set of overlapping circles – with the middle segment being the one that embodies your true calling. Before diving into each of the *ikigai* questions in detail, it can be helpful to undertake a similar exercise.

Draw three circles on a piece of paper, and next to each one, write down one of our three big questions: *What are you good at? What do you love? What does the world need?*[6]

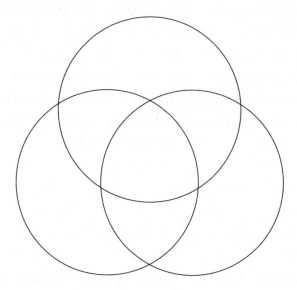

Inside each circle, write down a relevant experience – a positive moment in your job or a socially valuable role you hold in your community, say. For most people, there are only one or two experiences that sit in the middle of the diagram – the point where the three questions intersect. *Is this your ikigai? And what would it look like to build a life around experiences like these?*

WHAT ARE YOU GOOD AT?

Even though Rangan Chatterjee didn't learn the term *ikigai* until he was in his forties, in practice it had driven him for a long time. His upbringing in the Cheshire market town of Wilmslow instilled in him a ferocious drive from a young age. 'My mum and dad were immigrants to the UK in the 1960s and there was a lot of discrimination back then,' he explained. This led to a great focus on academic achievement. His parents' 'immigrant mentality', as he put it, led to a simple maxim: 'If you do well at school, you'll go to a good university and get a good job and life will be rosy.'

Rangan told us about his own father's background. Tarun Chatterjee moved to the UK from Kolkata in West Bengal to work as a consultant in genito-urinary medicine in a Manchester hospital.[7] His formidable work ethic meant he combined this demanding role with another – working night calls as a GP. For decades, he survived on just three nights' sleep a week.

Such demandingly high standards of work and commitment were passed on, implicitly and explicitly, to his son. 'I think for most of my life, I didn't feel good enough,' Rangan admitted to us. 'If I came home from school with 99 per cent, my mum and dad would say, "why didn't you get 100?" I took from that, if I'm not the best, if I'm not crushing it, if I'm not getting achievements, I'm not really loved.'

He acknowledged that his parents were simply doing their best by trying to help him be his best. 'I once spoke to Mum about it and asked why they had done that. "I knew you were capable and I wanted you to be the best that you could be," she

39

told me.' But the result of these exacting standards was that he soon began to push himself too hard.

In his late teens, Chatterjee left home to follow in his father's footsteps and study medicine. But he couldn't stop overexerting himself. He recounted the occasions in his student days in Edinburgh when his drive to excel would stray too far. Even if a casual game of pool wasn't going well, the disappointed voice of his parents – 'Why didn't you get 100 per cent?' – seemed to grow louder. He'd take a break, go into the toilets, and stare at his own reflection in the mirror before slapping himself across the face. 'If I was ever losing, I'd go and hit myself and say, "Come on Chatterjee, get back out there." More often than not, I'd go and win. But the pain of losing was too great.'

He never realised how harmful this relentless focus on excellence could be until he noticed the declining health of his own father. His dad, he told one reporter, 'killed himself working, chasing success, mistaking that for happiness'. His illness was long and protracted. 'I was living in Edinburgh when one night my mum called me,' he says, 'and this was out of the blue, at 10.30 at night, saying, "Listen, Rangan, you better come home now. Dad's in intensive care and I'm not sure he's going to make the night."'[8] His 59-year-old father's kidneys had unexpectedly failed.

As Rangan rushed down the motorway to Cheshire, he found himself reflecting not only on his dad's health but also on what really mattered in the end – and what it meant to live well. 'That influenced my entire adult life until nine years ago, when he died,' he once said.[9]

The death of his father led Chatterjee to question how he

was approaching his own life. 'When he died, it was a big hole in my life. For the first time in my adult life, I'd go walking and thinking,' Chatterjee says. 'I would question myself: *Am I happy? Whose life are you living? Are you living someone else's life? Or are you living your own life?* I asked myself a lot of existential questions.'

'Are you living someone else's life?
Or are you living your own life?'
Rangan Chatterjee

And this eventually led him to take a different route. After a lot of soul-searching, he eventually came to recognise that his own unique talents were not quite as straightforward as his parents had led him to believe. He was, at heart, an educator – a man with a unique passion to *share* his insights on how to help people live happier, healthier lives. This understanding was at the heart of his decision to write what became his best-selling books and record his phenomenally successful *Feel Better, Live More* podcast.

Chatterjee's life hints at how we can answer the first of our three *ikigai* questions: *What are you good at?* This is a question most of us ask ourselves at one time or another – particularly when choosing our career. But Chatterjee's experience shows it's not quite as simple as it sounds. Because being good at something isn't just about academic prowess or technical skill – it's also about alignment with your sense of self. How the things you *do* relate to your deepest sense of *who you are.* 'When you are not being authentic to who you are, you can't hide from yourself. It's really, really important.'

In this rendering, the question *What are you good at?* relates less to hard skills – writing emails, schmoozing clients, seeing patients – and more to the most profound questions of who you are. According to the psychologist Dean Keith Simonton,[10] talent is a 'package of personal characteristics that helps you acquire expertise or enhance your performance quickly in certain areas.' But to find these talents we need to reflect deeply on the things that make us feel fulfilled and which come easily. We tend to excel at these tasks because they align with our deepest sense of self.

So how can each of us find these natural talents? A good starting point is to look at the existing achievements from your life. But do not focus on the ones that have led to you being given the loudest acclaim or the biggest pay rises. Focus instead on those that have brought you pride.

Are there any moments from your past that make you glow when you think about them? Or memories that you always find yourself returning to when things are going wrong that make you feel better?

Next, like Chatterjee, compare these moments to what you currently do – and what you currently believe you excel at. *Does your current life bring you moments of pride? How closely aligned is what you do with what makes you feel fulfilled?*

This method hints at a more rounded way of thinking about what you are 'good at' than merely the cold, hard skills that are identified in the classroom or at work.

Talent is not just about what you are good at. It's about what gives you meaning. A sense of meaning that is the most powerful motivator in the world.

WHAT DO YOU LOVE?

Joe Wicks has the demeanour of a man who gets to spend all his life doing what he truly loves – and is smart enough to know it. His Tigger-like enthusiasm was infectious; as our conversation wore on, we found ourselves talking as loudly and quickly as the sports coach we were interviewing.

Little about Wicks's demeanour hinted at the difficulty of his early years – which were unimaginably distant from his current role as 'the nation's favourite fitness coach'. Wicks's mother Raquela was just seventeen when she had his brother, and just two years later Joe was born. His father Gary was a heroin addict, in and out of rehab for his crippling drug addiction. 'We had cheap plywood doors. My dad would punch through them or a wall when he and my mum were arguing. There was a lot of shouting, a lot of doors slammed,' he once explained.[11] 'Life was chaotic.'[12]

We were keen to understand how he had learned to identify his true passions amid these traumatic early experiences. 'We're all products of our upbringing, aren't we?' Wicks said. 'We have these experiences and they can really affect you.' In his case, his exposure to addiction frightened him. 'I'd heard once that you will be an addict if your father's an addict, as it's genetic. I had this fear that if I took drugs or drank, I was gonna become a drug addict.' This fear propelled him towards the gym. 'Because of that, I literally just channelled my energy somewhere else. I joined the gym at sixteen and it was like my therapy.'

Exercise was Wicks's escape then, as it is now. 'That was always the thing I fell back on,' he admitted to us. 'At school, it was the only subject that teachers could really truly tame me in because I was so distracted. I couldn't focus. Sport allowed me to run around and let off that energy, and that really fundamentally changed my life.'

Wicks didn't know it, but the seeds of his future life were being sown. 'I was a mini version of who I am now, rounding everybody up, telling them, "Come on, get changed, let's get out there – I can't play football without you! Get your arse in gear!",' he once said. 'That's been a massive part of my life.'[13]

In time, this led him to his true calling. After leaving school, Wicks took a sports science degree and then worked as a teaching assistant. But he didn't like the job. Before long, he says, he realised that he 'wasn't cut out for it'. And so he started asking himself some hard questions. 'I was like, "Right, what do I really *love* doing?" and that was exercise.' He left his teaching role and began working as a personal trainer, a job he did for five years. It was a new direction that would eventually change his life.

'What do I really *love* doing?'

Joe Wicks

During his time away from training, he began posting videos on social media of him cooking meals. 'No one that probably really loved cooking, like really skilful chefs, would have watched those,' he once told the *Guardian*.[14] 'They were for general people who just wanted to know where to start.' But his excitement and enthusiasm always shone through. By 2016, a million people were following him online. A publishing deal for his first book, *Lean in 15*, soon followed. It defied everyone's expectations by selling 700,000 copies – becoming one of the biggest selling cookery books ever in Britain. Wicks had sought out what he loved to do – and it had changed his life for ever.

Wicks's journey from troubled child to one of Britain's best-selling authors hints at how to answer our second *ikigai* question: *What do you love?* Simply reflecting on this question – just like Wicks did when working as a teaching assistant – can take us a step closer not only to happiness but also to greater creativity, good fortune and success.

To understand why, it's worth delving into a seminal 1998 paper by the psychologist Barbara Fredrickson entitled 'What Good Are Positive Emotions?'[15] As the title suggests, positive emotions are an evolutionary puzzle. Negative emotions have a clear biological benefit – prompting the famous 'fight or flight' sensation that will, say, stop you being eaten by a bear or bonked over the head by a Neanderthal with a club. Positive emotions have no such evolutionary effects. So why do we experience them at all?

The answer, according to Fredrickson, is that positive emotions tend to 'broaden and build' how we think and act. For example, the positive emotion of curiosity *broadens* the range of the ideas we will explore. When we are interested in something, it makes us want to pursue it, learn new things and tackle new experiences. The positive emotion of pride when we achieve something that matters *builds* what we think we can achieve, encouraging us to pursue even bigger goals. Positive emotions allow us to move from merely living to actively thriving.

That's why this second question is so profound. When we

focus on things that make us happy, we don't just feel better; we accomplish more too.

So take a moment to figure out what makes you happy. Sit down with a pen and paper and write down the answers to a few simple questions. *In what moments recently have you felt happiest?* Next, broaden it out to other positive emotions: *When have you felt most engaged, curious or excited? And what does all this tell you about what you love?*

By the time you finish, you should have a list of a few recurrent areas of your life that bring you true joy. Now, ask yourself what it would look like to integrate more of these moments into your life. *What would a life you really love look like?*

It's an irresistible way of looking at the world. As Joe Wicks bounced out of the High Performance studio, the effect of his *joie de vivre* seemed to hang in the air. His two interviewers looked at each other and laughed. 'Do you feel more enthusiastic than when we started?' Jake asked. 'I do.'

WHAT DOES THE WORLD NEED?

Susie Ma has a big, revolutionary idea: that we're getting purpose wrong.

'A purpose is different to a passion,' she told us on the podcast. 'You can be passionate about so many things but a purpose is what guides your passions and the decisions that you make.'

'A purpose is different to a passion.'

Susie Ma

We were only a few minutes into our interview with Ma, and it was already clear that she had a remarkable mind. Since walking into the room, she had already charmed us with her enthusiasm, wowed us with her articulacy, and vaguely alarmed us that she'd achieved so much before reaching her thirtieth birthday. Talk about showing up your interviewers, we thought.

Ma had founded her business, Tropic Skincare, when she was only fifteen, motivated by a desire to help her mother pay the bills and to buy her a big, beautiful house. When we sat down together seventeen years later, Tropic was one of the fastest-growing companies in the United Kingdom, with more than 3 million customers. Her mum was living in the house she had always dreamed of. And along the way, Ma had learned masses about what it means to create a business – and a life – with purpose.

Ma does not have the privileged backstory that characterises the early lives of many entrepreneurs. Born and raised as an only child in Shanghai, she spent her first few years in a home without electricity or heating. 'We didn't have the gadgets we have now, but it was happy,' she later told one interviewer. 'I had a great family and lots of love. I had everything I wanted. I suppose when you don't know what you could be having, you're happy with what you've got.'[16]

Her grandmother was an early inspiration. She was determined to raise the funds to allow her three children to move away from China and start a new life. 'She realised that the Western trend of wearing ties was becoming increasingly popular in Shanghai and she noticed all these poor Chinese men trying to dress up really nice, but they all had the same poor-quality ties.' She spotted the opportunity and acted decisively. 'She began making ties at home and then hustled, selling them at bus stops during really busy commuting hours.' The ingenuity eventually paid off. 'She was able to save up enough money to send my dad, my mum and me off to Australia.'

But the relocation wasn't easy. 'When I first arrived I was enrolled at a state school, and I didn't speak any English,' she once said. 'But one thing I was very good at was maths, because you don't need to know the language for that. Within five years – by now fluent in English – the precocious twelve-year-old was on the move again, relocating with her mother to London. 'I remember calling up the school and enrolling myself. They could tell that I was a little girl and asked to speak to my mum, but I said, "No!"'[17]

Ma was an academic child, leaving school with a slew of A* grades. But things weren't easy. The move from Australia to the UK had stretched her family's finances, and she would watch her mum often struggle to make ends meet. And that's how she began Tropic. She started working on a cosmetics stall at a local market as a means of helping with the bills. While there, she emulated her grandmother's entrepreneurial instincts from years earlier. 'I saw how much money I was making for the boss and how little he was paying me,' she would later recount.[18] And so she branched out on her own.

In the summer break between school and starting a degree at University College London, she began making a range of natural cosmetics, which she says were inspired by the botanical splendour of her childhood on the Australian coast. By the time her first term had begun, she had a product and a manufacturer in place. She spent her free time over the next few years selling a body scrub at her mum's toy and souvenir stall in Greenwich Market.

From the moment it launched, Ma's product was a runaway success. Soon, she had negotiated her way up from her mum's stall and into shops. She raised enough money to buy her mum a house, cover her university tuition fees and purchase her first investment property. And then – after her dream graduate job in a bank turned out to be less than she'd hoped for – Ma decided to put in an application to appear on *The Apprentice*. She not only breezed through the application process, but made it to the final of the show – impressing Lord Sugar, the host, with her tenacity and enterprise.

By the time the show went to air seven months later, Tropic was booming. Despite having 'fired' her less than a year previously, Lord Sugar put up a £200,000 investment for 50 per cent of the business – and she remains the only candidate to have received his financial investment without winning the programme. It's fair to say Lord Sugar's instincts have been vindicated: in 2021, Tropic turned over £90 million.

It was this dizzying ascent that first got Ma interested in the idea of purpose – and how we get it wrong. From her earliest entrepreneurial experiences, she had seen her business as answering a simple question: *What does the world need?* This question is the third ingredient of *ikigai* – but as Ma argued, it is also the one that's easiest to get wrong.

Ma noticed that when faced with this question, most of us are prone to think only of the short term. *What does the world need so I can make a quick buck? What does the world need so I can get the next promotion? What does the world need so I can pay my bills next month?*

But Ma was developing another way of thinking about

purpose – one she learned from the business author Simon Sinek. 'He introduced me to the idea of having an *infinite purpose*,' Ma explained to us. The concept – introduced in his book *The Infinite Game*[19] – emphasises the need to think about our impact beyond the short-term horizon; the need to think about the longest possible time horizon.

Sinek distinguishes between a 'finite mindset' and an 'infinite mindset' with a gaming analogy. Take chess: a game with a clear set of rules governing how you can move around the board, and a clear victor. Or take football: a game with a clear set of rules governing how you can play, and a winning side. 'These,' Sinek suggests 'are finite games, and they're centred around the self, competition, and our innate need to win.'[20]

In business, this mindset means focusing simply on short-term market gains. And yet it's a flawed way of thinking about business – and life. While we may aim to 'win' through these measurable results, the reality is that after each leader leaves, the game continues. 'In business, careers, politics and parenting, there's no such thing as an ultimate victor,' Sinek says. 'There's only the game itself.'

'There's no such thing as an ultimate victor. There's only the game itself.'
Simon Sinek

That's why the best businesses play the *infinite* game. They want to build something sustainable that will contribute to the welfare of staff, customers and communities in the long term. Their focus is not on now, but for ever.[21]

Ma rose to Sinek's challenge with enormous courage. 'I decided that my purpose – and Tropic's – was to help create a health*ier*, green*er*, more empowered Earth.' The suffix – *ier* and *er* – is crucial. 'This is infinite. There's always *more* green and *more* healthy.' It's an infinite purpose in action.

This change in perspective led to a transformation in how the company did business. Soon, Tropic began spearheading eco-friendly initiatives, such as opting for biodegradable ingredients in its haircare line. Suddenly, the goal wasn't hitting next year's profit target; it was making the world better. And this method is what took Tropic to even greater heights than it had before. At the time of writing, the brand is worth over £100 million.

You need not be in business to draw upon this idea. When someone asks, *What does the world need?*, the instinct is to think about the short-term horizon. This is natural. It's also a mistake.

When thinking about what the world needs, try instead to focus on the longer-term horizon. Ask yourself, *What will the world* always *require more of? What will people in 1,000 years' time look back on and think 'that was important'? What is my infinite purpose?*

This infinite purpose could take many forms. If you're trying to change your job, it might mean seeking out a role that makes the planet greener or fairer. If you're trying to transform your relationships, it might mean endeavouring to be kinder or more loving. If you're looking to excel in your creative pursuits, it might mean producing work that makes people happier and more fulfilled.

But in every case, look at the world not from the perspective of the finite you – focused on the next week or month – but the infinite you – focused on the for ever. *What is the biggest purpose you could serve? And how can you live up to it?*

LESSON SUMMARY

*Can you imagine a life that makes you happier
and makes the world better?*

- Before you can begin your change journey, you need to work out your end goal. The ancient Japanese art of *ikigai* – seeking out what you're good at, what you enjoy and what improves the world – offers a hint as to how.
- The first step to finding your *ikigai* involves asking: *What are you good at?* Think back to when you have felt both fulfilled and at ease – what does it tell you about the skills that come most naturally?
- The second step to finding your *ikigai* involves asking: *What do you love?* Reflect on the moments that have brought you the most joy – what would it look like to live a life with these moments at its centre?
- The final step to finding your *ikigai* involves asking: *What does the world need?* Reflect on your purpose, not today or tomorrow, but for ever – what would it mean to live a life focused on the infinite game?

Leap

If you don't face your fears, you'll never overcome them.

To dream, know who you are. To leap, know where you are.

THE POWER OF WHERE YOU ARE

There was a huge, under-acknowledged player contributing to Alex Scott's success. A player that nobody, except her, seemed to appreciate.

In a career that spanned three separate spells at Arsenal and three years in America, Scott had become the face of women's football. A crucial player in Arsenal's record-breaking 2006–07 season, she had also been part of the first English team to win the UEFA Women's Cup (scoring the deciding goal in the last minute of the first leg), ultimately playing for England 140 times across four European Championships and three World Cups. Oh, and then seamlessly transitioning to a career in TV. It made your authors feel a little inadequate, frankly.

And yet throughout the interview – and our conversation – Scott displayed no ego whatsoever. She was at pains to point out that what she'd achieved was only partly due to her astonishing talent and hard work. And at every turn, there was another factor at play: her environment.

One of the most striking themes of her remarkable book

How (Not) to Be Strong is its focus on how, whenever things were going wrong, Scott had a remarkable knack for seeking out environments in which she would be able to thrive once more.[1] Near the start of the book, for example, she recounts the troubled relationship between her parents. It was not an easy upbringing. 'From when I was a baby I could feel it, the environment we're in,' she writes. 'If you step out of line you know what's going to happen and you don't want that to happen.' From a young age, however, this environment was something she tried to change. She would escape to the football cages – 'my happy place' – near her home. 'I felt fun, I felt free and at home I was locked in, it was an environment where it was very much controlled,' she once observed.[2]

Later, when she went to Arsenal, this ability to seek out uplifting environments remained key to her success. The Arsenal Women manager Vic Akers had scouted her at eight years old, impressed by her ability to dazzle the boys she played football against in the cages.[3] Akers would often help young players find second jobs, knowing they were paid a mere £50 a match. Scott was offered a job in the Arsenal laundry room. Where some might have recoiled at the prospect (it seems unlikely such a role would have been expected of an up-and-coming male Arsenal player), Scott again saw it as an opportunity to take control of her surroundings. 'It's easy to go to the negative situation and think I'm in a laundry, I'm scrubbing dirty pants,' she said. 'Actually that environment allowed me to learn so much. I was in a football environment. I was having conversations with Arsène Wenger and I'm having conversations with Thierry Henry about football.' Her overriding memory was how educational the experience was, she says.

Later, Scott would again seize the opportunity to transform

her environment – embracing the challenges of US football (or 'soccer', perhaps). In 2008, Scott was approached about joining the US side Boston Breakers to play in the National Women's Soccer League (NWSL), widely regarded as the best in the world. She was encouraged not to take the role. 'People were telling me, "You can't go to America; you're not gonna play,"' she said. But she knew right away that she would learn so much from the environment. 'The biggest lesson that I learned in America,' she said, 'was the mentality of why the American team has been so successful. They know they need everyone to be good at the level to ultimately win.' She took this lesson in leadership and was able to apply it within the England national team.

All in all, Scott's focus was on putting herself in an environment in which she could thrive. 'Creating the right environment is key,' she says; 'creating an environment where everyone feels valued and that their part matters to the whole success of the team. I think that's the biggest thing.'

'Creating the right environment is key.'
Alex Scott

Scott's observations are in keeping with work conducted in the earliest days of modern psychology. In 1936, the psychologist Kurt Lewin coined one of the most famous equations in the social sciences:

$$B = f(P, E)$$

In simple terms, it states that a person's behaviour (B) is a function (f) of their pre-existing personality (P) combined with their environment (E).[4] Or, put even more simply: what we do depends on where we are.

This is an important lesson if you want to change your life. In this section, we're moving from imagining another life to jumping headlong into it. It's a scary moment; but if you don't face your fears, you'll never overcome them.

However, as Lewin acknowledged, the key to successful change lies in your surroundings. To dream, know who you are. To leap, know where you are. The focus of the Leap section, then, is on your environment – and whether it really sets you up for success.

HOW TO FEEL SAFE

What are the components of a positive environment?

To answer that question, let's take a visit to the West Yorkshire town of Dewsbury. It was 14 December 2009, and Sam Burgess' life was about to change for ever. He had spent his life in the area and was playing in rugby league's premier competition, the Super League, by the age of seventeen – all while nursing his father through his battle with the unutterably cruel illness of motor neurone disease (MND).

But the tender care and sensitivity he showed towards his father stood in stark contrast with his burgeoning professional reputation. He quickly became renowned for his unrelenting toughness, playing rugby league the old-fashioned way: hard. He sought no favours and didn't dispense many either. By his twenties, he had caught the eye of Hollywood superstar Russell

Crowe – the co-owner of the South Sydney Rabbitohs. When Burgess signed for the Rabbitohs on his twenty-first birthday, he was catapulted into the top tier of global rugby.

For the first time in his career, he was scared. 'I went from being the hunter to being the hunted,' he told us. 'I knew that because I'm English, I play for South Sydney – a huge club – and Russell Crowe has brought me to Australia, I had a target on my back . . . I had a friend of mine warn me, "Listen, they are going to come for you. They're going to come and try and bash you."'

And yet he got through it. How? The answer lay in the environment that Crowe offered him. 'We were playing a trial game at Redfern, which is the club's spiritual home, and it was a sell-out, and I was starting to get nervous,' Burgess recounts. As he was completing his final warm-up, Crowe knocked on the door and beckoned him. 'He walked me on to the field, around the back of the sticks, before he pulled out of his pocket a membership card with my father's name written on it along with some of the phrases he used to say to me before each game.'

He then pointed at an empty seat in the stands – a seat next to his own. Crowe had bought the seat for his father and promised it would remain forever empty in tribute to him. 'If you're ever in doubt or you want to see him, just look to that seat. It'll be in the stadium for ever,' Crowe said.

'I just didn't expect it,' Burgess recalls. 'It was a really over-powering, emotional experience that I couldn't control. I just burst into tears on the field.'

Years later, he would say that this moment transformed his relationship with his professional environment. 'How can I not be connected to the club?' he asked himself.

When we spoke to Burgess on the podcast, he credited that moment with helping transform his career. Burgess made his mentor a promise: to win Australia's National Rugby League (NRL) Grand Final for the first time since 1971. 'I told him, I want to turn your team into a winning team.' It took him five years and some Herculean efforts – but in the fifth year of his Australian adventure, he was able to honour that commitment in the most remarkable manner possible. Burgess played almost the entire 2014 Grand Final with a fractured cheekbone and eye socket. His right eye was swollen shut, and his cheek blown up like a balloon – but Burgess played so well in a crushing 30–6 defeat of Canterbury Bulldogs that he was still awarded man of the match.

Burgess's experience with Crowe hints at the first way we can rebuild our environment – and so begin to change our life. As Burgess and Alex Scott have shown, our brains are constantly scanning where we are to determine whether there is anything that might present either a threat to our safety or the opportunity of a reward for us to enjoy. In fact, our brains are estimated to do this, on average, around five times per second.[5]

Anything that is associated with positive emotions and rewards – such as being seen, heard and listened to – will trigger an *approach response*; we want more of it, and we will move towards where it is being offered. Conversely, anything that may contain a negative emotion or experience – such as being ignored, dismissed or rejected – will be interpreted as a threat and trigger a powerful *avoidance response*, where we hesitate and make excuses not to take action.

This is known as the 'minimise danger, maximise rewards' response; according to the neuroscientist Evian Gordon, it is 'the fundamental organising principle of the brain'.[6] And it is why our environment is so important: when our environment feels safe, we thrive. When our environment feels dangerous, we fail.

So how can we create a safe environment, just like Russell Crowe did in Sydney? One in which we feel at ease and ready to take the leap into a better life? In the following two lessons, we'll be outlining a simple set of characteristics that create safety – which, handily enough, spell SAFE:

- Status
- Autonomy
- Friendship
- Equity

The first two – the focus of Lesson 3 – are about transforming *where you are*: ensuring you're in a *place* to change your life. The second two – the focus of Lesson 4 – are about transforming *who you're with*: ensuring your relationships are strong enough for you to make that leap. Between them, they add up to a four-step method for transforming your environment.

SEEK STATUS

The first step to creating a safe environment can be gleaned from the surprising life story of Josh Warrington.

As a schoolboy, Warrington had been a respectable amateur boxer – but due to a series of narrow defeats and near misses at key moments, he never achieved the dream he had nursed since first entering the sport: boxing for his country. Disillusioned with the amateur game, Warrington decided to push through his disappointment and take a chance to join the sport's professional ranks. There was just one problem: he was only sixteen. The sport's rules decreed he had to be eighteen to box for a living.

'I managed to come out of school with eleven GCSEs, all A–C passes, but then I was like, *what do I do with myself now?* It was two years before I could turn pro,' he told one journalist. 'Some of my friends had ideas of going to university, so they were off to college. Others were going to work for family businesses or do a bit of labour work. They had their future mapped out, whereas I didn't have a clue what I wanted to do.'[7]

After a few months of doing nothing much, his dad helped find him a job he enjoyed – working in a local dental laboratory. By the time his three-month trial period was over, Warrington's boss realised he was on to a winner – and that Warrington's fearsome work ethic and sharp mind made him an excellent fit for the role. He told Warrington he wanted to keep him on in a more senior role. The issue was, to progress from the lowly ranks of dental assistant, he needed to become fully qualified. And that meant going to university for the next four years. His boss offered to pay on one condition: that Warrington fully commit to the studies.

And so began an exhausting new routine: working in the dental surgery during the day, boxing in the evenings and studying at night. His weeks soon resembled a logistical obstacle course – and while Warrington skilfully dodged every obstacle, that came at the expense of any meaningful social life. As he sought to maintain his relationship with Natasha, his soon-to-be wife, he struggled to keep himself motivated. 'At one stage I thought *something's got to give. I can't do all this*,' he later recalled.[8]

But what made it worse was the jealousy. In addition to his punishing schedule, Warrington was watching his friends go out at the weekends and party. According to an intriguing profile of Warrington in the *Athletic*, everything came to a head one Friday night when he called round to the house of one of his friends to deliver tickets for an imminent fight. The group were gearing up to attend a big twenty-first birthday party of a mutual pal. Warrington told his mate how envious he was of his old friends.[9]

What happened next would change Warrington's life. 'My mate, who normally talks a lot of shit and is constantly telling the worst jokes in world, all of a sudden decided to give me a life lesson,' Warrington told us. '"Listen, mate," he said. "We've been doing the same thing for the last three years, since we're eighteen. We are the same people, going to the same places, doing the same thing. It's fucking boring."'

He paused before delivering the knockout blow.

'"Let me tell you now, from my point of view and from anyone else who looks at you, we think: *How does he do it?* We all look at you and wish we had carried on like you. I could have been somewhere – somewhere you are now. Everyone's proud of you. You're doing really well."'[10]

When Warrington recounted these words, he seemed more emotional than at any other time in the interview. He was revealing how his friend's acknowledgement of what he had achieved had encouraged him to keep on trying – when otherwise he might never have persevered. 'I don't underestimate the importance of when my friend reminded me to stay true to my ambitions,' he told us. And it worked. By the time he became European champion (during his nineteenth pro fight) and then World champion (in his twenty-seventh fight), Warrington was headlining shows on television – all while still working in the dental laboratory three days a week.

'I don't underestimate the importance of when my friend reminded me to stay true to my ambitions.'

Josh Warrington

Why did this little intervention from his friend have such a stark impact on Warrington? To understand it, we need to realise how our social brains are calibrated to assess how our behaviour can diminish or enhance our status. When we are afforded a high – or enhanced – social status, it impacts our health and longevity of life. We don't just crave recognition, we live or die by it.

The trouble is, status is difficult to assess objectively. We can understand how difficult it is with a short thought experiment, which the psychologist Richard Wiseman brilliantly explains in his book *The Luck Factor*.[11] Let's pretend that you are an Olympic athlete. You turn up to your first ever games and win a bronze medal. How happy would you feel? If your answer includes words such as 'ecstatic', 'thrilled' and 'proud', you'd be right.

Now run the thought experiment again. The situation is the same, but with one crucial difference: this time round, you win a *silver* medal. How happy would you feel? The logical answer is that the silver medallist would be in a better mood than the bronze medallist. Unfortunately, in that you would be completely wrong.

Research indicates that those who won a bronze medal are often far happier than those who win silver. The reason has nothing to do with their actual status – and much more to do with the way in which they *think* about their status. 'The silver medallists focus on the notion that, if they had performed slightly better, then they would have won a gold medal,' explains Wiseman. 'In contrast, the bronze medallists tended to focus on the thought that if they had performed slightly worse, then they wouldn't have won anything at all.'[12]

This intriguing study hints at why Josh Warrington's friend had such a transformative impact on his life – and teaches us all something important. We crave status – but we're no good at appraising it without bias. Think of those bronze and silver medallists.

And so we need to put ourselves in environments where people make us feel good – where they tell us we're doing well, emphasise our achievements, make us remember what we're best at. This is where Josh's friend came in. Those simple words – 'You're doing really well' – were enough to bolster his sense of status and in turn, his sense of safety.

There's a lesson here for the rest of us. Most of us have worked or lived in environments in which everyone is always down on us and our skills: there's a lack of praise and even less excitement. And most of us have also spent time in environments where everyone is constantly reminding each other how talented, kind and handsome we are: they are defined by high fives, congratulations and praise.

The former environments are draining. The latter are inspiring. And if we want to achieve a true sense of safety, we should seek out these positive environments wherever possible. They hold the key to feeling safe – and in turn, making the positive changes we seek.

PITSTOP - THREE SUPPORT NETWORKS

As Josh Warrington found, placing yourself in a supportive, status-bolstering environment is crucial to changing your life. The trouble is, it's not always clear what such an environment looks like.

When psychologists talk about support systems, they are talking about three distinct forces – each important but each subtly different. There's *emotional support*: things like encouragement, empathy and love that are most likely to come from the people you love. There's *instrumental support*: meeting your physical needs, be that a sandwich, a cup of tea, or a new laptop. And there's *informational support*: providing guidance, information and mentoring.

Most of us have encountered all three at one point or another. In the spaces below, write down three places where you receive each form of support. Next, reflect on what that says about what your environment offers you and what it doesn't. *Are there some forms of support in which you feel you're lacking? If so, how might you go about finding them?*[13]

Emotional support

1. _____

2. _____

3. _____

Instrumental support

1. _____

2. _____

3. _____

Informational support

1. _____

2. _____

3. _____

OBTAIN AUTONOMY

Have you heard about the Olympic swimming champion who was allergic to chlorine?

This is not the start of a joke. It was instead the start of our discussion with Australia's greatest ever swimmer, Ian Thorpe – a man whose allergy to chlorine was only one of the many surprises he had in store for us.

The first surprise was that, despite growing up as the son of a talented Australian cricketer and an accomplished netball player, he discovered at a young age that he was useless at ball sports. He was, according to his father, 'a chubby lad' who 'had no eye-to-hand coordination at all at a very young age'. He liked cricket and football; but, alas, he didn't have an iota of talent for them.[14]

So he followed his sister's lead and went to the swimming pool instead. After becoming 'sick of watching Christina compete at swimming carnivals' he decided he wanted to give it a try himself.[15] It was at this point that he took the plunge. And promptly discovered his chlorine allergy.

Instead of dissuading him from trying, though, the allergy brought out the first signs of a hitherto hidden competitive streak. Wearing a protective nose clip and swimming with his head above the water, he developed an unconventional style – one that was soon paying dividends. In his first competitive swim, he came home in first place. He enjoyed the feeling and wanted to experience it again. Soon, he was spending increasing amounts of his spare time in the pool – and rapidly becoming a talented athlete.

If his parents were disappointed that Ian had the makings of a swimmer, not a cricketer, they didn't show it. He told us that it was his parents who helped his initial spark of enthusiasm catch fire. 'My parents were exceptional in terms of what is appropriate for someone that is a talented young athlete,' he said. 'They knew what to do and what not to do.'

His father's recommendation? If he and his sister wanted to become exceptional, they would abide by two simple rules. First, *commitment*. When they agreed to participate in a sport, they had to make a go of it for a whole season. 'No matter what we took out, whether it was good or bad, we had to finish the season. At the end of each season, it was up to us whether or not we wanted to continue,' Thorpe recounted.

Second – and, for our purposes, more importantly – *autonomy*. Every individual in the family was responsible for their own success. 'I had to wake up at 4.17 in the morning,' Ian told us about his training routine. 'It was then up to me to actually wake my parents.' This focus on autonomy was key to his ultimate triumph. 'Most parents find themselves waking their children and being the catalyst,' he says. 'But it's on the athlete to be ready, not on their parents. I don't think that they should set the alarm clock.'

'It's on the athlete to be ready.'

Ian Thorpe

This distinction – of learning to wake up for yourself, rather than being woken up – is a powerful glimpse into the second strand of building an environment that supports us in our change journeys. Psychologists have long understood that environments in which we have little control over what we do and how we do it are unlikely to elicit positive change. Even the *perception* of reduced autonomy, such as being micromanaged or given too many rules to follow or being woken from our slumbers by our parents, can generate a threat response. The neuroscientist Steven Maier has shown in a wide range of studies that whenever animals are placed in stressful situations, the most important indicator as to whether they can function effectively is the degree of control available.[16]

The flipside is that when we do have autonomy over our

decisions, we are massively more able to effect the changes we seek. In his book *Stumbling on Happiness*, the psychologist Daniel Gilbert describes a study of nursing homes from the 1970s that shows why. All of the nursing home residents were presented with the gift of a houseplant. Half of them were told that they were in charge of caring for the plant; the rest were told that a member of staff would take care of the plant for them. A small difference, perhaps. And yet, Gilbert writes, 'six months later, 30 per cent of the low-control group had died, compared with only 15 per cent of the residents in the high-control group.'[17] The lesson: residents who were given more control over their decision-making lived longer than those who didn't have the same autonomy.

This hints at why Ian Thorpe's training method was so powerful. By being given autonomy over his routine, his method and his training, he developed a great sense of independence – one that led to massive success. It would ultimately lead him to swimming immortality.

Because Thorpe's emphasis on autonomy did not just make him more committed. It also made him more creative – giving him an approach to swimming quite unlike any of his rivals.

This was in fact a method that first became apparent when he was fifteen and went up against his fellow Australian, Grant Hackett, in the 1998 World Championships. A couple of years older, Hackett had established dominance in the 400-metre freestyle in general and over Thorpe in particular. But this time was different. With 100 metres left to swim in the final, Hackett was comfortably leading. And then Thorpe tried something new. In the final straight, Thorpe executed a finishing burst of unprecedented speed. One spectator described it as 'a kick that looked like someone had attached an outboard motor to his feet'. With metres to go, he overtook Hackett. At fifteen years and three months old, Thorpe was the sport's youngest-ever male world champion.

This distinctive approach would take Thorpe to greatness. The next year, he smashed the 400-metre freestyle world record by two seconds – a victory that Rowdy Gaines, a three-time Olympic gold medallist, attributed to his approach to the finish. '[Thorpe] went into a balls-out sprint at 250,' Gaines said. 'I have never seen anything like that.'[18] And between the 2000 and 2004 Olympics, Thorpe would take home nine medals – including five golds.

Thorpe's enormous emphasis on autonomy – in his training routine, in his method, and in his life – holds a lesson for us all. If we want to change ourselves, we need to seek out environments in which we have autonomy: just like in Thorpe's household, where he'd get up and only then wake his parents. And you can readily apply his insight to your own life.

Ask yourself: *How much autonomy do you have over your routine, your job and your relationships? And what would it look like to exercise more control than you do currently – waking up five minutes early, cooking your own lunch, completing that task in your own way?*

All too often, we think we have no control over our environment. Usually, we're wrong. We can always take control of some aspect of our environment – it just takes a little creative thought.

LESSON SUMMARY

Will the place you are in support you in making the changes you seek – and if not, why not?

- Where we are has a profound impact on what we do. Our environments can set us up for happiness or despair, success or failure. If we want to leap into a new life, we first need to take control of our environment.
- The primary way our environments determine our behaviour is obvious: where we are. Our jobs, our houses, our communities – these are the forces that determine what sort of changes are possible.
- Humans are status-obsessed. And so the first way we can change where we are is by seeking out environments that bolster our sense of status. *Where do you feel most at ease about your position in the group?*
- We also crave autonomy. So the second way to change where we are is by seeking out environments in which we have a sense of control. *In what moments do you have the greatest sense of agency over your situation?*

Changing your world means finding your people.

THE POWER OF WHO YOU'RE WITH

There was a brief moment of silence. And then the crowd erupted.

It was the 2016 Olympic men's 100 metres breaststroke final in Rio de Janeiro, and Britain's Adam Peaty had just crossed the finish line. For a moment, people didn't quite believe it: not only had he won the gold medal, he had demolished the world record in the process.

But if the crowd was going wild for Peaty and only Peaty, he was at pains to point out that his success was in large part due to others. When he saw Mel Marshall after the race, the 21-year-old placed his gold medal around her neck: it is '50 per cent yours', he told her.[1] For the past seven years, she had stood by his side every step of the way.

Formerly a professional swimmer, Marshall had worked as a community swimming coach before eventually being appointed head coach at the City of Derby club. This community coaching mentality meant she had an egalitarian mindset. Everyone got the same treatment. 'You're gonna go to your Olympics, whatever that might be,' as she puts it. 'That might be the county championships; that might actually be the Olympic Games. There's no ceilings, there's no boundaries.' Her only demands were enthusiasm and commitment.

Above all, Marshall emphasised the importance of one factor: relationships. 'You look at the pyramids,' she laughed. 'There wasn't a spreadsheet used there. It was getting all these people in one place with a great vision . . . to make something impossible happen,' she explained to us. 'That's what we all go to work for: human connectivity.'

'That's what we all go to work for: human connectivity.' Mel Marshall

This emphasis on connectivity would take her coaching career to greatness. Shortly after beginning coaching, Marshall had a meeting with a mortgage adviser. It was a routine visit, but one that would take her life in an unexpected direction. The adviser's son had a friend at his local swimming club called Adam who was decent, he said. Marshall suggested he come along to Derby. When the fourteen-year-old Peaty arrived, Marshall watched his freestyle and was distinctly unimpressed. And yet when he started doing breaststroke, it was like watching a completely different athlete; she knew immediately he was special. From that moment, Marshall resolved to be his coach.

After she first saw Peaty's breaststroke, Marshall recounts telling Ross Davenport, the recently retired double Commonwealth champion: 'Ross, I'm telling you now, this kid is going to win an Olympic medal.'[2] That would turn out to be an understatement. By the summer of 2016, when Peaty was twenty-one, he had amassed three World Championship gold medals, eight European Championship golds and two more at the Commonwealth Games. In April 2015, he set a new world record at the British Championships, before adding the 50 metres world record to his trophy cabinet in Russia two years later. The only title missing from his treasure chest was the Olympic gold – and it was soon being discussed in the media as a question of 'when' not 'if'.

For the young Peaty, the weight of expectation went from heavy to intolerable. But it was in this moment that Marshall's emphasis on relationships became invaluable. Marshall took it upon herself to create a video montage for Peaty in advance of his trip – a series of tributes from friends, family and anyone else who had backed Derby's greatest swimmer in his journey. It was a reminder that relationships matter. 'We had the heart of a community supporting us, and I did this for him,' Marshall later said. 'It came to him that I've done alright here: I've come a long way.'[3]

While the bright glare of an Olympic spotlight can cause some to wilt, it made Peaty come alive. He set a world record in the heats, followed by a similarly blistering semi-final win. While waiting in the call room for the final, Marshall whispered a reminder to 'burn your boats'. 'If you're going to go out, go out in style and do it how you want to do it.'

And that's just what he did. After the race, Marshall sent Peaty a text. 'As the sun sets on the history you have made, enjoy every second,' she wrote. 'Breathe it in and know that it's yours forever ... It's been an honour. Well done, Olympic champ.'[4]

The powerful bond between Marshall and Peaty hints at the second way to create a safe, nurturing environment. In the last lesson, we learned about how to transform *where we are*: by seeking out places that bolster our sense of status and autonomy. In this lesson, we turn to how to transform *who we're with*. The trick to an uplifting environment, as we'll see, also lies in crafting positive relationships.

According to Naomi Eisenberger, a social psychologist at UCLA, relationships are some of the most powerful forces in the world.[5] In one experiment, Professor Eisenberger and her colleagues created a computerised ball-tossing game called Cyberball, designed to simulate the feelings caused by strong and weak social bonds – before using brain scans to look deep into the heads of those who played, as they played.

The rules of the game were very simple. Each volunteer was paired with two other 'people' (who were actually avatar simulations from the computer program) and told to 'catch' the ball – which they did by pushing a button at the correct moment. In the first round, all the participants received a fair number of passes. But in the second round, Eisenberger made a subtle change: the real-life participant was ignored and completely excluded from being passed the ball.

The impact of this small tweak was significant. Even though everyone knew the avatars were computer-generated, researchers found 'a pattern of activations very similar to those found in studies of physical pain emerged during social exclusion, providing evidence that the experience and regulation of social and physical pain share a common neuroanatomical basis'.[6]

Being left out activated the same neural pathways as being punched.

What this study – and countless others – demonstrate is that the brain is a social organ, hugely dependent on strong relationships. We are told as kids that 'Sticks and stones may break my bones, but words will never hurt me.' The science suggests otherwise. In fact, the feeling of being socially excluded is one of the most painful stings imaginable.

The flip side is just as powerful. When we seek out nurturing, caring relationships – ones that make us feel at ease and happy – we are vastly more likely to feel good about ourselves and, in turn, feel able to change our situation.

And that's important. Because it means that changing your world means finding your people.

FORGE FRIENDSHIPS

Our best insight into how to build powerful social connections comes from an unexpected fusion of reality TV and scientific research. Exhibit A: *Geordie Shore* superstar Vicky Pattison. Exhibit B: a famous social psychology experiment undertaken in 1970s Boston.

When we sat down with Pattison on the *High Performance* podcast, she had yet to turn thirty-five but had already been in the public eye for a decade. Pattison made her TV debut on *Geordie Shore* aged just twenty-three. She spent the next few years on screens in various states of drunkenness, often polarising viewers into two camps: those who hated her and those who were still in the process of making their minds up. 'I showed some really ugly traits,' she told us. 'I was defensive, aggressive and angry. I became this caricature of what I thought everybody wanted – this really bolshie Geordie girl . . . I lost myself totally.' Her most notable moments on the show and in the tabloids were when she was filmed having sex under a duvet and being arrested for attacking two women in a nightclub (not at the same time, we hasten to add).

And yet when we spoke to Pattison for the podcast, she was like a different person. She had just published a book about her journey, *The Secret to Happy*.[7] And a lot of that secret seemed to relate to a simple lesson she'd learned: knowing who your friends are.

It hadn't been a straightforward journey. After leaving *Geordie Shore* in 2014, Pattison had jumped aboard the reality show merry-go-round – a journey that culminated with her 2015 appearance on the fifteenth series of *I'm a Celebrity . . . Get Me Out of Here!* 'I thought I might not be a popular choice,' she later admitted to the *Daily Mail*. 'But as I was waiting to go into the camp, incommunicado, I was blissfully unaware that social media was going crazy, demanding I be axed from the show.'[8]

And yet she won people round – eventually being crowned Queen of the Jungle in the final public vote. This was not her happy ending, though. Upon her return, Pattison signed up for a TV documentary that offered viewers the inside track on her marriage preparations with her fiancé, the businessman John Noble. During the recording, she discovered that her fiancé had cheated on her while on holiday in Dubai – a story that was gleefully splashed across the tabloids. 'It was awful, heart-breaking,' she would later explain. 'I felt destroyed.'[9]

So how did Pattison come back from it? The answer, it seemed, related to rethinking her approach to the people around her. Where she had once relished antagonising people – and the tabloid attention that came from doing so – she learned to respect the people around her. She came to understand the transformative power of friendship.

Pattison told us that in the wake of this, her worst moment, she developed a new way of thinking about the people around her. You can work out who is a real friend by dividing the people around you into a few simple groups – using what she calls 'the phone test'. 'There are three types of people in life, and you can work out who they are by how you feel when they ring your phone,' she explained.

Group one are the 'draggers' – 'those people who, when you see their name like flash up on your display screen, you think, *For fuck's sake.*' It's a sensation Pattison knew well. 'When I first moved to London, I had friends who would ring me, and I just knew they would be after something. "I need somewhere to stay," they'd say, or "I need tickets to this." They would never call because they were genuinely interested in me, to check I was happy.' These people, Pattison says, were to be avoided.

Next come the 'middle-of-the-roaders'. 'When they ring, you sort of think, *Mmm, should I answer? Should I not? OK, I'll pick up.* They don't set your world on fire but they're perfectly nice.' This group 'don't understand where you are going but you don't need them to. They get where they fit in your life – they're kind, mean well and have their hearts in the right place.' It's easy to dismiss these people, but they're important, she says. 'They make you feel OK, they don't rock the boat and they don't give or take to your overall mood.'

But the real key to good relationships lies in group three: the 'igniters'. 'We should all strive to be igniters; the kind of person that when you see their name pop up on your screen, you can't wait to answer. They make you buzz like an old fridge,' she says. This group of 'magical, shiny people' has been invaluable in allowing Pattison to thrive in the face of endless public judgements. She credits her igniters for helping her through her worst times in the wake of her very public break-up – and getting her back on her feet.

'We should all strive to be igniters.'
Vicky Pattison

Pattison might not have known it, but her taxonomy of friendship was mirroring one of the most famous ideas in the history of psychiatry. Long before she discovered the perils of going on *Geordie Shore*, the psychologist David Kantor had undertaken an experiment that has been described as 'the first incarnation of reality TV' – and it gave him an intriguing take on how humans interact.[10]

It was the early 1970s and Kantor was a lecturer at Tufts University – with a particular interest in new approaches to treating mental illness. The medical profession was in the throes of a revolution in how it approached mental illness, and Kantor was one of many who wanted greater emphasis placed on how it was society, as much as the inner lives of individual patients, that made people ill. This approach led him to devise an elaborate experiment to study how schizophrenia manifests not within specific patients, but within groups. He asked a handful of families with schizophrenic members for permission to set up cameras in various rooms of people's houses.

Kantor soon detected a surprising pattern within the behaviour of every group, including those without any schizophrenia present. After analysing the tapes, Kantor concluded that each individual within a family unit will fall into one of four roles.

First are the initiators: the person who always has the ideas for everyone else to follow – from what to do with a weekend to what to have for dinner.

The second group do precisely the inverse. These are the blockers. Whatever new idea the initiator comes up with, the blocker finds problems with it. If the initiators energise us to go and embrace new ideas, spending a similar amount of time with blockers has the opposite effect, making us reluctant to do anything.

The third group are the supporters: who tend to take one side or the other, but rarely initiate any given decision. Finally, there are detached observers – 'who stay disengaged and neutral, tending to merely comment on what is going on.'[11]

Kantor's point wasn't that any of these four approaches are 'good' or 'bad'. Although the 'blockers' might sound doom and gloom, they can actually be quite important in ensuring the group continues to function – having to endlessly say 'yes' to everything might be no fun at all. In fact, the most successful groups tend to be made up of many of the different types – just like Pattison's embrace of both the 'igniters' and the 'middle-of-the-roaders', as she put it.

As such, Kantor's theory allows us to build a well-balanced society – with people who fulfil every role that you need for a social group to succeed. It invites us to ask ourselves: *Who are the initiators, blockers, supporters and observers in my life? Do I have the right balance of people who encourage me and people who remind me of the risks? What is each one of my friends bringing to the table?*

Finding the right balance of these social types can be transformative. It allows us to forge friendships in which we feel more at ease, in which we make better decisions, and in which we are able to leap into the new life that we seek.

PITSTOP – THE FOUR-PLAYER MODEL

In the boxes below, write down the names of the initiators, blockers, supporters and observers in your life. *What do you spot? Do you have a well-balanced group of friends – and if not, how might you find more of the 'players' who you lack?*[12]

Initiator – *active, supportive, helpful, filled with suggestions*	Blocker – *troubleshoots, identifies obstacles and highlights potential difficulties*
Supporter – *always sides with one group or another*	Observer – *not bothered in the slightest*

EMBRACE EQUITY

By themselves, friendships are not enough to nurture a safe environment for change. These friendships need to take the right form. And that's where the final ingredient in our SAFE equation comes in: equity.

The importance of social environments that are fair is best demonstrated by Bear Grylls. We invited Bear on to the *High Performance* podcast to celebrate our 100th episode and assumed the subject matter of the conversation would be extreme. We had spent hours watching footage of him drinking his own bodily fluids, eating elephant dung and scaling Everest. So imagine our surprise when we actually got a masterclass in the basics of everyday relationships. Grylls spoke to us about the enduring importance of humility, social connection – and above all, fairness.

'The currency at school tends to be about celebrating the sporty or the academic or maybe even the good-looking,' he told us. 'Those are the things that carry weight at school but count for very little in life; the currency of life is the opposite of that. It's resilience and a positivity and a never-give-up spirit.' It was this approach, he said, that drove his every success. 'The one muscle you need in life is the inner muscle of the never-give-up, resilient muscle.'

Grylls should know. His CV is adorned with accomplishments made possible by his astonishing resilience. In 1996, aged twenty-one, his parachute failed to deploy on a training mission and he broke his back. 'I should have cut the main parachute and gone to the reserve but thought there was time to resolve the problem,' he told one interviewer.[13] Facing three broken vertebrae, he was not expected to make a full recovery. And yet he did. 'I was within a whisker of not being able to walk again . . . So I have gratitude for life. I feel I've been given a second chance. What life asks of me is to live it with positivity and boldness.'[14] Eighteen months later, he would reach the summit of Everest.

But this NGU – never give up – spirit is not something that comes about by itself. Grylls told us that at every turn, his ability to accomplish things was down to the social environment in which he placed himself. And above all, finding relationships that place an enormous premium on one quality: *fairness*.

He cited one military exploit as an example of the importance of building fair relationships. 'Chris Carter was my first sergeant when I first joined my SAS squadron,' he said. 'He was a giant of a man; gruff, opinionated, hard but kind. Above all, he was fair, and this was a real influence on me, especially as a young soldier. He looked out for the right people at the right time.'

'He looked out for the right people at the right time.' Bear Grylls

Grylls' voice began to crack when he recounted the experience that would most influence his own approach to leadership. 'We were in the desert together and were waiting for a resupply of equipment and water, which was three days overdue. We were out of water and hiding in an LUP (lying up point) which was boiling hot. We had been rationing our water and I finished mine while Chris had been much smarter and rationed well.'

'We had a long, twenty-kilometre march to get to the helicopter at night and I was really struggling at this point,' Grylls later said. 'I will never forget what he did next. We were six hours into this extraction and he just quietly took me aside and made me take his last cap of his water, which at that stage was as valuable as gold.

'He didn't do this in front of anyone, and initially I resisted. I said: "No, I've got it, I've got it, I'm good." He simply said, "drink the water" and with that tiny little cap, he gave me more strength than any water ever could.'

That moment has stayed with Grylls. 'Chris sadly lost his life in Afghanistan but for me, he's immortal,' he once said. 'I always remember that moment and I told it to his family, many years later. I don't remember him for his fighting or his all-round brilliance but for his kindness. I have always tried to live with a little bit of his spirit in me.'[15]

The powerful effects Chris had on Grylls' outlook are underpinned by the astonishing psychological power of feeling like someone is dealing with us fairly. The importance of fairness to the human psyche is supported by one of the most well-known experiments in the field of behavioural economics: the 'ultimatum game'.

The premise of the ultimatum game is that two people must agree a way to divide £10.[16] Each participant has a different role, however. First, the 'proposer' makes an offer – say, £9 for me and £1 for you. Next, it falls to the 'responder' to either accept the offer or reject it – in which case both players leave with nothing.

In theory, the 'responder' will accept any offer – even if it's just a penny. If they accept, they will get some money, and if they reject, they get none. And so a 'rational' proposer will offer as little money as possible to their partner. It makes perfect rational sense.

Except in practice, this isn't what happens. Low offers almost always get rejected. People would rather give up free money than accept what they perceive as inequitable behaviour – in which the proposer is hoarding all the money for themselves. Intriguingly, the proposers tend to guess that this will happen – and so behave in a relatively generous way. For which reason a completely equal 50–50 split is the most common offer made. And the psychological effects are powerful. As Golnaz Tabibnia, a professor at UCLA and an expert on the 'ultimatum game', puts it: 'Receiving a fair offer activates the same brain circuitry as when we eat craved food, win money or see a beautiful face.'[17]

This hints at the final ingredient of finding powerful social environments. The places in which we are able to thrive – and the people who bring out that thriving in us – tend to be those in which we are treated with generosity and fairness.

So if you want to find a nurturing environment – one in which you can live up to your best self – try to seek out people who treat you equitably. Those who respect you and treat you as an equal. Those who would, you suspect, give you a fiver in the ultimatum game – or offer you their last sip of water.

Grylls put it most succinctly: 'Kindness is king. There's no point getting to the top of that mountain in life – whatever that mountain is, whether it's getting a degree, or starting a business, or whatever – if you're an arsehole.'[18]

LESSON SUMMARY

How do the people around you inform your behaviour – and do they set you up to succeed or fail?

- Relationships are one of the most powerful forces in the world. The people we're with have a huge impact on what we do. If we're serious about change, we must seek out social environments that bring out our best characteristics.
- That starts by embracing the revolutionary power of friendships. Friends – real friends – invite us to think clearly, act creatively and take measured risks. They will encourage us to change, even when it feels hard.
- And it continues by bringing a powerful sense of equity to every relationship that we craft. When we are treated fairly, our minds feel at ease and our behaviour is more considered – the perfect bedrock for beginning the fight to transform ourselves.

Fight

Everyone faces setbacks. Your job is to surmount them.

When things are disintegrating, hope is the one constant.

THE OBSTACLES TO CHANGE

Tyson Fury is a fighter. And in more ways than you think.

When we travelled to meet the heavyweight champion of the world in his home town of Morecambe, Lancashire, the 6 foot 9 giant arrived dripping with sweat, following an early morning run. He meant business. 'I don't do many of these interviews,' he declared. 'Let's get it on.'[1]

As the conversation progressed, we realised why he agreed to so few of them. It was a draining experience in its emotional intensity. 'I've had to face a lot of shit and trauma in my life,' he told us. 'I have become very comfortable going into the most uncomfortable circumstances. If you can learn to do that, then that's where you're going to be successful or have high performance in your own area.'

Some aspects of Fury's story are well known – from his long struggles with mental illness to his astonishing 2015 ascent to become world heavyweight champion. But the thing he most wanted to talk about was the aftermath of that great victory. A period that would prove to be the greatest fight of his life.

In November of that year, Fury had beaten Wladimir Klitschko in Germany to become the world heavyweight champion. The fall back to earth began almost immediately. On the podcast, Fury described to us returning to his hotel the night of his victory. 'I remember just lying thinking, *I hope this isn't a dream.* I was lying there with my eyes open, and I couldn't sleep. I was thinking, *I will be fulfilled if I die right now. I don't have any more purpose in my life. I've achieved my life-long dream.*'

Fury was twenty-seven and had accomplished everything he set out to: finding a family, money and fame. 'I had everything,' he said. 'But from that moment, for the next sixteen months, there wasn't one day that went by that I didn't want to die or wish death upon myself.'

This is when trouble set in. 'Robbie Williams later told me that it's called Paradise Syndrome,' Fury said, a condition sometimes ascribed to individuals who have accumulated such significant success that they no longer feel they have anything left in life to accomplish. Fury was a classic case. He admitted that his ambition – 'this impossible dream to beat Klitschko and become champion' – had helped him keep his struggles with mental illness in check. Dream realised, his life had disintegrated.

'I got lost in between these two characters: Tyson Fury, who is a husband, a father, a son, a mental health patient and a guy who, who's interested in boxing,' Fury recalls. 'He's a very flawed character. Very normal, fat, bald and lazy at times. I then have the Gypsy King, who has never, ever suffered with any problems or had any complications in his life. That person is unbeatable. These two got entangled and I couldn't tell them apart . . . It was very, very hard for me and I was lost and couldn't get out.'

The three years after winning the title and achieving his childhood dream were horrendous for Fury and his loved ones. He was suffering panic attacks and wasn't finding joy in anything – not even boxing. In his lowest moment, he seriously considered suicide. 'I bought a brand new Ferrari convertible. I got the car up to 190mph and heading towards a bridge,' he said in one interview. 'I didn't care about nothing, I just wanted to die so bad.'[2]

And then he thought again. A voice came to him, Fury told us. 'It said: "Don't do this. Think about your kids growing up with no dad." I pulled over. My heart was beating out of my body; tears coming down my face and I was hyperventilating.

'That was the moment that I knew I had to go see the doctors straight away,' he said.

Fury's recovery was not easy; in fact, it's an ongoing process. By early 2018, he had found that medication and embracing regular exercise were helpful. This slowly ignited a renewed interest in boxing – the focus on which helped Fury manage his addictions. He got back into fighting shape and he came back into the ring for two successful fights.

Then, in December 2018, he did something extraordinary. After publicly sharing the trauma of his depression in a raw and moving documentary, he agreed to a fight with the man who had acceded to his throne in his absence, the unbeaten Deontay Wilder. Everybody said that Fury – out of shape and not having had a serious fight in three years – stood no chance. They didn't reckon with the Gypsy King.

In front of an awestruck 18,000-strong audience in Los Angeles, Fury outboxed Wilder over eleven gruelling rounds – until disaster struck in the last one. He dropped like a fallen tree, his head hitting the canvas. He looked like he was out cold. Wilder made a throat-slitting gesture in celebration while Fury lay limply on his side. But then the impossible happened. As the referee's count reached six, Fury stirred and started to move. At eight, he began to push himself back up to his feet. It was impossible to escape the metaphor for his own journey back to life.

Unfathomably, Fury ended the fight in utter control. Wilder resorted to desperately clinging to the edge of the ring. The bout was ruled a draw – but Fury subsequently proved his superiority by knocking out Wilder twice in their two rematches. It was an astonishing comeback from a man who only months previously had been at his lowest ebb.

Fury's story is a parable about the third step in the journey to changing your life. So far, we've explored how to identify a better life (Dream) and take the first jump into realising it (Leap). But now you're in for the hardest part of your journey: the Fight stage.

When you embark on a change journey, it's common to feel highly energised and motivated at the beginning – and to feel the same way as you reach the end. It is in the middle stages – what the author Brené Brown refers to as the 'messy middle'[3] – where the real struggle happens. Think of Fury at his lowest moment, still a long way from realising his dream – returning to full health and beating Wilder. Here, everything feels like a failure – and the ending still remains alarmingly distant.

According to Rosabeth Moss Kanter, a Harvard-based professor of business, this is the hardest part of any change journey. 'The middle includes those moments when it seems you can't move forward. You don't feel comfortable. The goal seems far away. In the middle, we all have doubts – even the true believers.' In a study of hundreds of major changes, both personal and professional, she found that this is the point at which people are disproportionately likely to abandon hope.[4]

But there is a solution. In the middle of Tyson Fury's journey, he thought about giving up – the barriers to returning to form simply seemed too great. But he managed to overcome each one of these obstacles and, in turn, realise his wildest ambitions.

We can all follow his lead. In this lesson, we'll delve into the three greatest barriers we encounter – fear, uncertainty and doubt – and explain how each one of them can be overcome. Everyone faces setbacks. Your job is to surmount them.

Because one point is certain: When things are disintegrating, hope is the one constant. However hard you fall, there is always a way to pick yourself up from the floor of the ring.

FACE FEAR

Seven hundred and forty-four days.

Just over two years. Just under 18,000 hours. And the length of time between two of the most significant landmarks in the modern history of English football. The first of these dates, 27 June 2016, marks what is commonly regarded as the lowest point in England's recent footballing past: when the national team ignominiously crashed out of that year's European Championship in France at the first knockout stage with a dispiriting 2–1 defeat to Iceland, a country with a population of under 400,000.

The second date, 11 July 2018, heralds England's appearance in the World Cup semi-final against Croatia, the furthest the team had ventured in the tournament since England's heartbreaking defeat by West Germany in 1990.

What had changed? How was it that a team that lacked all inspiration and confidence – who had, as the joke went, been 'beaten by a country with more volcanoes than professional football players' – become one of the most impressive squads in the world in only two years?

When answering these questions, it's tempting to start by looking at what was added to the team. Was it the arrival of a new head coach, Gareth Southgate? That certainly made a difference. But one man alone could not transform a team so quickly – this was, after all, a man whose only stint in club management had until then entailed leading Middlesbrough to relegation.

Or was it an influx of younger, more talented players? Perhaps. But while England played, sounded and looked like a completely different team to the one that had left France humiliated, nine of the fourteen players who were involved against Iceland were still present 744 days later.

Rather than looking at what was added, the change could be better attributed to looking at what was taken away. Namely, one distinguishing factor that had hamstrung so many elite performers whenever they pulled on their national jersey: a force that, according to Southgate, hung 'heavy' on their backs. We are talking about *fear*.

Fear is the life's work of Dr Pippa Grange, who in 2017 was appointed by the Football Association as its head of people and team development. Tasked with building the resilience of the squad in the face of intense media scrutiny, she chose to focus on creating a sense of safety.

In her book *Fear Less*, Grange explains precisely why she thinks fear is such a malign force.[5] 'There are two types of fear that we all experience,' she says. 'The first is "in the moment" fear.' This is best understood in those moments when a truck is bearing down on you and you need to get out of the way. This kind of fear, she explained, is an evolutionary necessity. It is invaluable for our very survival.

But there's a second type of fear which is altogether more insidious. This is the 'not good enough' fear, which is both bigger and broader and is one of the biggest obstacles standing in our way of making change happen. 'This,' says Grange, 'takes much longer to control.' It often shows up as perfectionism or self-loathing – unhelpful forces whether you're trying to build a new skill, work on a relationships or, say, beat Iceland's football team.

This type of fear is the greatest obstacle in the fight to change our lives. It does us no real good. But it can be eliminated.

How? Well, in the course of our fascinating discussion, Grange offered us a three-step remedy for addressing the 'not good enough' fear. A method she called 'see, face, replace.'

The first step is *seeing your fear*. This is a simple step – and involves little more than asking yourself, *What am I actually scared of?* Take a moment to stop and think – and even write down – what is making you feel so on edge. One helpful method that Grange offers her clients is encouraging them to describe their fears in visual terms. She doesn't mean as an abstract set of sensations but as a physical thing; perhaps a beast with eyes, claws and a nose, or a dark cloud hanging over your head. 'An image has texture and tone that maybe language doesn't always possess,' she has said.[6] The more vivid the image, the clearer your impression of your fears will be.

The second step is *facing your fear*. Try to build an even clearer picture of your fear; the more detail the better. Again, here, it can be helpful to ask yourself some simple questions. *What is it that makes this task so scary? Is it triggering memories of past negative experiences? Is it that the task looks too difficult, that the deadline is too soon, or that the people involved look too intimidating?* Again, stop and write down your answers. Can you get a clear, detailed sense of the problem before you?

Finally, and most importantly, comes step three: *replacing your fear*. In her book, Grange says that once we have a clear sense of what we're scared of, we can begin to replace it with something else: whether that's a good laugh, or a sense of passion. How? Well, one of her methods is to begin writing 'a different story' for ourselves. 'Narratives inform us in extraordinarily dramatic ways, and I feel that perhaps we don't realise how often we have the pen in our own hand around those narratives,' she has said.[7] You can't change your circumstances. But you can change your story.

'Narratives inform us in extraordinarily dramatic ways.' Pippa Grange

So take a moment to stop and ask yourself: *What would a more uplifting narrative about this fear look like? What would it look like if I were the type of person who could overcome this obstacle? How would I be feeling and what would I be thinking? And is there a way to embody this new version of 'me' right away?*

Having heard Grange's method first-hand, we started to realise that – much more than any change in the team or manager – this method is what explained the turning around of England's performance. Suddenly, theirs was a culture without fear. For example, in the aftermath of England's march to the World Cup semi-final, Gareth Southgate emphasised his focus on what the players were telling themselves about what they were scared of. 'We've spoken to the players about writing their own stories,'[8] he said. That involved getting the players to sit down together in small groups to share their life experiences and anxieties and to reveal intimate truths about their character and what drives them. The point, Southgate said, was to build trust, 'making them closer, with a better understanding of each other'.[9]

This approach helped the players see their fears clearly for the first time. To face them and truly understand where they came from. And above all, to replace them with a new story: one that focused less on fear and more on possibility.

It worked. When, in 2018, the team upended years of failure in penalty shoot-outs by beating Colombia, Southgate explained why facing and replacing fear was what had made all the difference. 'Tonight they showed they don't have to conform to what's gone before,' Southgate said. 'We always have to believe in what is possible in life and not be hindered by history or expectations.'[10]

PITSTOP - VISUALISE YOUR FEAR

We admit it: neither of your two authors have ever been much good as artists. So we probably weren't the likeliest candidates to be lured in by Pippa Grange's invitation to draw our fears on a piece of paper. At first, we were too shy about putting our fears down in such vivid terms – not to mention that our children had, we suspected, overtaken us in the artistic arena.

But we have been forced to admit it: sketching out your problems really does help. According to Grange, this is 'a way of allowing more descriptive material, more of the unconscious and the tone of things to come through in what somebody is sharing.' And it works. By putting pen to paper, you start to think about – indeed, to see – your problems from completely different perspectives.

And so in the boxes, we've offered you some spaces to draw your fears from different spheres of your life. Don't feel self-conscious. Just draw without thinking, and see what comes to light. By the end, you might just have a different understanding of the obstacles you face.

Your biggest profes-sional problem . . . *as a monster.*	Your greatest romantic concern . . . *as a landscape.*
Your greatest fear about the future . . . *as a person.*	Your most long-standing self-doubt . . . *as a building.*

UNDO UNCERTAINTY

Eddie Jones spent his childhood never quite fitting in.

The son of a Japanese-American mother and Australian father, he grew up in a suburb of Sydney where his background made him stand out. There were around thirty children in his school class, he told the podcast *Life Lessons: From Sport and Beyond*.[11] 'Twenty-six Anglo-Saxons, three aboriginal kids and myself.' Jones went on to recount how his mother encouraged the traditional Japanese custom of bringing friends presents when he visited their houses. As a child he found even this small difference mortifying. 'Other people could never understand why that was done. So, you were different.'

This feeling of being the odd man out would follow Jones through his career. Despite playing against the British and Irish Lions for New South Wales B in 1989, that was as far as he went: he never made it into Australia's first team. Some critics over the years have suggested this chastening experience left the perennial outsider with a point to prove: a consistently recurring theme of his entire coaching career. As he recognised after being appointed to the top England job in 2015, he would always be an outsider. 'I'm an Australian coaching in England rugby,' he has said. He was, in the words of one newspaper profile, 'England's outsider'.[12]

But what the young Jones could not have realised was that this outsider status would eventually give him his superpower. When he was given the top England job, his critics suggested he would be a short-term stand-in, unlikely to last in what was a notoriously difficult job. And yet, when we sat down with him, he was approaching his sixth year in the role. How come? The answer, we came to suspect, is that his background gave him a unique ability to spot someone who was feeling unsure about their role – and offer ways to make them feel more confident.

Soon after joining England, Jones decided that three players – James Haskell, Dylan Hartley and Chris Robshaw – were going to be integral to his plans. This was a controversial move: none had shone in the 2015 World Cup – Hartley even had to miss the tournament because of a ban. But Jones thought he could see raw talent; these men just needed a coach with the vision to unlock it.

He was particularly interested in one of them. 'James Haskell made enough noise for the whole squad,' Jones writes in his memoir.[13] 'I initially suspected that [he] was quite an insecure character who tried to hide his vulnerabilities by making a racket and kidding around.' It was precisely the kind of outsider status that Jones recognised in himself. 'He just wanted to be loved,' Jones said.

Jones was right, as Haskell himself would go on to admit. He had spent his entire career feeling uncertain of his position, he once suggested. 'I was never that comfortable,' he recalled of the time before Jones joined the team. 'I'd get one game and have a man-of-the-match performance, or near enough, and be dropped the next week. The coaches would say: "We never drop a man after a really good game" and I'd say: "What happened there? With me?" They'd say: "Fair point but . . ." I don't think they understood how to get the best out of me.'[14]

This inconsistent approach generated uncertainty and prevented Haskell doing his actual job. He obsessed over how his every action might derail his standing and his position. 'It eats away at you – 100 per cent,' Haskell said. 'I've always been confident in my rugby ability but with England I had to adjust my behaviour.'[15] Just when he should have been fighting at his hardest for the England team, he was feeling insecure and demoralised.

And then Jones arrived. 'Haskell wasn't brave enough to be himself,' Jones told us. 'What I tried to do was get him to be himself.' Above all else, that meant giving Haskell the confidence to give up on the comedy and develop a sense of certainty about his status in the team. 'At the start of 2016 Six Nations, I guaranteed him a spot for the whole tournament,' Jones said. 'I wanted to make him believe in himself and also take a bit of pressure off him, as well.'

'I wanted to make him believe in himself.' Eddie Jones

The effect of this decision on the player was both instant and powerful. 'I went into an environment where I really felt respected for the first time,' Haskell later said. 'People talked to me like an adult, they wanted my opinion and that gave me the confidence to play. I felt empowered. I didn't feel I was walking a tightrope where, after one mistake, I'd be slung straight out.'[16]

Jones' intervention was only small. And yet it worked wonders. Over the next two seasons, Haskell delivered dazzling and unprecedented performances. His greatest moment came during the victorious 3–0 whitewash series against Australia in the summer of 2016. Haskell was deservedly recognised by his fellow players as 'man of the series' for presiding over the total decimation of Australia's illustrious back row. He was a player transformed.

How was it that this simple vote of confidence from Eddie Jones was able to transform Haskell's performance?

The answer, perhaps, relates to how the brain adapts to uncertainty. The science is clear: the human mind loathes ambiguity. In our favourite study on this subject, volunteers were given the chance to answer three quiz questions – and offered a reward for their efforts. But first, they had to make a choice. They could either be told the correct answers to the questions and whether they had got them right or wrong; *or* they would receive a chocolate bar but never hear the correct answers. The thing is, not everyone was given the same version of the experiment. Some volunteers were given the chance to pick their reward *before* they took the quiz, others only *afterwards*.

The results were intriguing. When given the choice *before* the questions were asked, most people picked the chocolate bar. But the group given it *after* hearing the questions were much more likely to opt for the answers. In other words, once they had engaged with the task, uncertainty became something they simply couldn't bear – to the extent they were happy to sacrifice a reward to eliminate it.[17] The human mind loathes uncertainty. It will do anything to remove it.

Why do we struggle so much with uncertainty? Well, when your brain is confronted with any kind of doubt or ambiguity, your subconscious flashes up an alert signal: *Pay attention! There may be a threat!* This kind of alert is something that must be fixed before we can feel settled again. George Loewenstein, a behavioural economist at Carnegie Mellon

University in Pittsburgh, describes the pain that uncertainty causes us as 'a mental itch, like a mosquito bite on the brain'.[18] This makes it harder to perform at our best. Uncertainty stops us concentrating. It stops us multitasking. And it stops us taking the risks required to succeed.

This was precisely what was going on in Haskell's head before Jones took the helm of the England team. He was never confident in his position, and so he could never relax. And because he could never relax, he could never play as well as he might. By eradicating this uncertainty, Jones transformed him into a star player.

So, uncertainty is the second big obstacle to change – particularly when you are in the Fight stage. You have probably experienced this yourself. Have you ever struggled to apply for a promotion because you don't feel confident enough in the job you're currently in – even though all the evidence is that you're performing well? Or failed to build a new relationship because you're feeling anxious about it ending at any moment? In both cases, uncertainty is acting as a blocker to the changes you seek. It happens to us all.

But this obstacle too can be surmounted – and with relative ease. The trick lies in giving yourself a vote of confidence – just like Jones gave Haskell.

DESTROY DOUBT

As soon as Liverpool FC's captain Jordan Henderson had lifted the Champions League trophy in June 2019, his first thought was to seek out his father, Brian. They had both scaled their own mountains to meet at this summit.

Over the previous few years, Brian had successfully battled throat cancer; and during the same period, Jordan had battled crippling doubt – from within and without – to take his club to the pinnacle of European football. Nothing about the journey had been easy. For Henderson, the Fight stage for him had been defined by vicious public criticism, disillusionment, heartbreak and the very real prospect of being sold to Fulham – all while his dad fought a life-threatening illness. His resilience through it all made him the living embodiment of what his celebrated coach, Jürgen Klopp, had meant when he declared his mission for Liverpool: 'to change doubters to believers'.[19]

Few people realised quite how difficult things had become for Henderson. When we sat down for the podcast, he told us about how much of his career had been defined by indescribable pressure – which was exacerbated by a set of unhelpful beliefs about how to overcome stress. Born and raised in Sunderland, Henderson described the local culture in his autobiography: 'Where I'm from ... you just get on with it, if things are hard. I want to help other people, but I'm not good at accepting help. I always put a shield up around myself.'[20]

It's an approach that will eventually take its toll. 'When I was coming home, back then, I wasn't in a great mood a lot of the time,' Henderson has said of his difficult early years at the club. 'I was still very young and learning how to deal with situations like that.'[21] Everyone could see that Henderson had the potential to be a world-beating player. But they could also see that he was struggling.

One day, in a moment of desperation, he decided to seek out the company of Dr Steve Peters, the psychiatrist who was then working at the club. 'I ended up speaking to Steve quite regularly,' Henderson told us. Peters was already famous as the man who had transformed the culture of British cycling. He was the man who the multi-gold-medal-winning Olympian Chris Hoy had, in a previous episode, told us was responsible for his every success.[22] And his method is simple. To first focus not on our behaviours but on our beliefs. Because what we *believe* about ourselves is a key factor in determining our outcomes.

A good example is Father Christmas. Do you remember when you were first told about Santa Claus? The story was probably imparted with some dire warning that the likelihood of him deciding to come down your chimney depended upon a combination of what you believe and what you do. If you believe in him, he comes; if you disbelieve, he doesn't. And if you're nice, he comes; if you're naughty, he doesn't. If you were to put this into a simple formula, it would read:

Your beliefs + your behaviour = result

Crucially, here, it's the *belief* in Father Christmas that actually leads to the change in behaviour. If you believe that he is going to arrive bearing gifts at the house of well-behaved children, it becomes entirely logical to change your actions in response. Changed beliefs lead to changed behaviour. Changed behaviour leads to changed results.

Adult behaviour is very similar. What we believe about ourselves informs our actions; and our actions are what ultimately determine our outcomes.

This insight – which we first encountered via Chris Hoy – would have a transformative effect on Henderson. It is one of the lessons that Peters would impart to the young footballer. And it offered him a way to change his beliefs – and in turn change his behaviour. With time, Peters helped Henderson see that holding on to his old beliefs – *I just get on with it if things are hard. I always put a shield up around myself* – was an obstacle to his success. This belief that he had to be the strong, silent type – the man who couldn't and wouldn't reach out for help – was standing in his way. It was an insight that would help lead him to that Champions League trophy.

Our harmful beliefs, then, are the third great obstacle to change. Along with fear and uncertainty, our beliefs lead us astray. Consider the following: *Have you ever decided against getting help with a task because you thought it might make you look weak? Or decided that a difficult task is simply impossible and given up before you've even started? Or told yourself that someone really doesn't like you, so there's no point making a social effort with them?*

All of these are harmful beliefs that we allow ourselves to entertain. They inform our behaviour and, in turn, dramatically change our results. But the thing is, like Jordan Henderson, these stories can be changed. It's possible to choose a better narrative about how the world is: rearranging your thoughts, beliefs and actions to get a different – and more positive – result.

How? One of our favourite methods involves sitting down and assessing how true the things you're telling yourself actually are. Next time you're bumping up against a belief that's holding you back – 'those people don't like me' or 'I can't do that task' – grab a pen and paper and do the unthinkable: write it down.

In the first instance, be as frustrated, negative and miserable as you like. Don't hold back, put it all down in writing: 'I saw them laughing about me at the Christmas party'; 'I tried to take the first step and couldn't do it.' But the next step is to be a little more optimistic. Try to balance things up a bit. Write down if there's another way to see it: 'I only heard a bit of that conversation, it could have been about anything'; 'I've completed similar tasks before, and it was hard but I managed to pull it off.' Finally, read through each statement and ask yourself a simple question. Is this true, false, or don't you know?

Now take a step back and look at your overall score. *How true is your belief? And is there another way to look at it?*

In our experience, this exercise is a powerful way to break through the negative patterns of thought that hold us all back. We all convince ourselves of things that aren't true. *Nobody likes me. I can't do it.* But we all have the ability to transform those beliefs into something positive. And when we do, the fight to change becomes a little easier.

LESSON SUMMARY

What are the biggest obstacles standing between who you are and who you want to be – and how can you surmount them?

- The Fight stage will be the hardest part of your change journey. This is the 'messy middle', the moment when you have embarked on your pursuit of a new life – but it still feels alarmingly distant.
- You can struggle through the Fight stage by identifying the biggest obstacles you face – and eliminating them one by one. First up, *fear.* Identify the scary truths you're telling yourself – and get to know them so you can, in turn, replace them.
- Second, there is *uncertainty.* When we are unsure of our standing, it becomes near impossible to fight on. But when we give ourselves little boosts of confidence – reminding ourselves of all we have achieved and all we will go on to achieve – we can replace uncertainty with confidence.
- Finally, eradicate *doubt.* We all doubt ourselves sometimes – but often these doubts are harmful misbeliefs rather than the truth. By taking a step back and appraising what your skills really are, you will give yourself the chance to fight another day.

We all face
setbacks. The
question is how
we interpret them.

REFRAME SETBACKS

After he was diagnosed with terminal motor neurone disease, Rob Burrow introduced a 'no-tears policy'. His wife Lindsey proved much better at sticking to it than we did.

Lindsey was telling us about the weeks and months that followed his diagnosis, almost a decade into their marriage. 'I took the kids swimming right after we had been told,' she says. 'I just sat, numb with shock.' It was only days later that the tsunami of emotions – grief, anger and regret – hit her with full force. Distraught, she forgot her PIN number at an ATM and burst into tears. 'I was breaking down,' she recalled in one interview.[1]

But Rob had a remarkable knack for seeing the positive. 'Rob was a tower of strength,' Lindsey says. 'He would say, "Pull yourself together and we'll deal with it." It was a wake-up call in many ways.' He had a unique way of putting things in perspective. 'I thought, *if Rob can be so positive and he's the one that's going through this, I need to stay positive for him.*'

Lindsey's interview on the *High Performance* podcast was probably the most moving – and, yes, tearful – we have ever undertaken. Indomitable and inspiring, Lindsey spent almost an hour explaining the lessons she had learned about developing a sense of perspective and maintaining a positive outlook – and how she applied those abilities in the most harrowing circumstances.

The couple had met when Lindsey was just twelve and were childhood sweethearts. Two decades later, they were as in love as ever, enjoying a happy and loving marriage in Leeds with three children, Macy, Maya and Jackson. Lindsey worked as a physiotherapist; Rob played for Leeds Rhinos, with whom he had won eight Grand Finals and established himself as one of the greatest rugby league players of his generation.

And then, in December 2019, their lives were turned upside down. At the age of thirty-seven, Rob was told he had just a few years to live. Suddenly, Lindsey faced a future without the love of her life, raising their young children without a father.

Yet Lindsey remained remarkably strong. How? The answer lies in how the pair reframed what had happened to them. Lindsey told us how Rob suggested they frequently take time to consider how lucky they had been for so long. 'Life is for living and it is so precious. Even in times of adversity, we can still be happy,' she told us.

 'Even in times of adversity, we can still be happy.' Lindsey Burrow

This optimistic mindset does not come naturally. Lindsey

explained to us how she forced herself to focus on how she could deliberately affect her own mood. 'There are days when you think: *Why me?*' she told one interviewer. 'But then I think of Rob and that really puts it into perspective because I'm able to physically do what I want . . . I look at Rob and think: *What have I got to moan about when he stays so positive?* What I have to do is nothing compared to what Rob goes through on a daily basis.'[2]

Above all, the two have learned to focus on how lucky they are to have known one another in their prime. 'Rob is such a wonderful man and I am the person I am because of him. So the good absolutely outweighs the bad,' Lindsey says. 'I still love every minute we have together.'[3]

Lindsey and Rob offer a powerful insight into how to respond to adversity. Most of us, thank God, will never experience a situation as horrific as his diagnosis. But that doesn't mean we can't learn from the pair. The pair offer an example for anyone who will ever experience setbacks – in other words, all of us.

All too often, when faced with setbacks, we become fatalistic. You're feeling low today so conclude you'll feel low for ever. Or you have an argument with your partner and conclude that your relationship is over. Humans love to seek out evidence for the negative – and conclude from it that everything will always be wrong.

Lindsey and Rob hint at another way. They demonstrate that when things go wrong, you can always find a way to reframe your experiences in a positive light. And when you're in the Fight stage of your change journey, that's a lesson you need more than ever. We all face setbacks. The question is how we interpret them.

So reframing setbacks is the focus of Lesson 6. Here, we'll identify three techniques that our high performers have used to see the bright side in even the hardest circumstances. It will show that even in the night's darkest moments there is always light, sometimes just beyond the horizon.

GAIN PERSPECTIVE

What would you do if you discovered that your partner had been cheating on you? And what advice would you offer to your best friend if they discovered their partner had been cheating on them?

Spend a few moments reflecting on each of these questions – and then reflect on your two answers. Was the advice any different in each case?

If so, you've just experienced the effects of 'Solomon's paradox' – so named after the biblical king renowned for his wisdom about everything apart from his own life decisions.[4] The phenomenon was identified in a fascinating study into human decision-making by the psychologist Igor Grossmann.

A researcher at the University of Waterloo in Ontario, Canada, Grossmann was interested in the difference between the advice we give others and the advice we follow ourselves. So he designed an innovative experiment. He divided 100 students in long-term relationships into two groups. The first group was asked to imagine being cheated on by their partner. The second group was asked to imagine that it was their best friend who had been cheated on. Next, both groups were asked questions to determine their ability to respond effectively to this situation.

The results were striking: the students advising themselves sucked; the students advising others excelled. Those who had imagined their friend being cheated on scored much higher on 'wise reasoning', appraising the situation with greater insight than those who imagined they had been cheated on. As Grossmann put it, his results 'demonstrate a new type of bias within ourselves when it comes to wise reasoning about an interpersonal relationship dilemma'.[5]

Solomon's paradox is not limited to our romantic lives. It crops up again and again when we encounter difficulties. When we experience a problem ourselves – whether we've been cheated on, lost our job, or failed an exam – our emotions sabotage our ability to see clearly. In these moments, we are the worst person in the world to give us advice. We need to get outside of ourselves.

But how? One answer comes from the highly charged world of Formula 1, an arena in which any momentary lapse of judgement could put you in mortal danger. Christian Horner, the head of the highly successful Red Bull team, explained to us how he managed to ensure that his team members maintained a sense of perspective – by encouraging them to get out of their own heads and into other people's.

In the world of F1, clashes between drivers are common, even within the same team. Despite sharing a crew, each driver is also fighting for a spot on the podium. It created a peculiar dynamic in which drivers are both team-mates and rivals.

Horner told us that his job was to prevent this environment from leading to clashes between his drivers. 'It's about being clear that there's no room for egos here,' he said. 'You know, it's all about teamwork; it's about working for each other and not just as an individual.'

'It's about working for each other and not just as an individual.' Christian Horner

It would take all Horner's skill to realise this ideal. Between 2010 and 2013, Horner's Red Bull team were consistently finishing in first position – winning four consecutive constructors' and drivers' titles with the charismatic German Sebastian Vettel behind the wheel. But things weren't easy. In 2010, Vettel was joined on the team by Mark Webber, a fiery, competitive Australian who also had a shot at winning the title. Webber once admitted to us that he found the team environment difficult: 'It's really, really challenging from a managing perspective because you get a divide within the organisation,' he said. 'Tensions went very, very high.'

These tensions resulted in a number of fractious incidents involving Vettel and Webber. 'Relatively early on in their relationship, they were starting to get pretty feisty with each other,' Horner told us. First, in a race in Malaysia, the German driver deliberately ignored the team's orders to snatch victory from Webber. Later, things boiled over at the 2010 Turkish Grand Prix – where the team's two drivers collided with each other and cost the team a 1–2 finish.

Horner realised that he had a problem. Both drivers were so blinkered by their own ambitions that they were harming their own chances, not to mention those of the team. It was a classic case of Solomon's paradox. They were so over-invested in their rivalry that they couldn't see what was best for themselves.

So Horner decided something had to change. 'I thought, I need to deflate this, I need to put things into perspective here,' he told us. And so he staged an intervention. Horner's idea was to invite both drivers to a meeting. But the location was designed to shift their perspective – away from themselves and towards other people.

Horner's venue of choice? Great Ormond Street Hospital for Children, London.

Before the meeting between the two drivers, Horner arranged a morning where both drivers spent time on the wards. 'I got both drivers to meet some of the kids and parents that were having a tough time, facing heartache in real-life issues.'

The intended effect was to remind both men to get some perspective – and get out of their own heads. 'We've got it pretty good,' Horner said he wanted the men to think, 'compared with the challenges and the anguish that these poor children and their parents have.' And it worked. 'After that we had a period where there was a reasonable level of respect between the two of them,' he said. 'It still boiled over at some points . . . But it was a good reminder.'

Horner's method hints at how we can stop obsessing over our own problems – and instead see them from the perspective of the people around us. It was a classic solution to Solomon's paradox: force the two men to stop obsessing over their own petty rivalry and see things as clearly as a friend – or even stranger – might.

You can apply this method in your own life, without the need for a hospital visit. Like Horner, try to do something that gets you out of your own head – and into someone else's. That might involve a visit to a children's hospital, yes; but it might also be as simple as watching a film, reading a book, talking to some strangers in a park. Even better, try describing the problem to yourself in the third person. On the podcast,

Rangan Chatterjee put us on to some research by the noted psychologist Ethan Kross, suggesting that speaking to ourselves as another person helps us get out of our heads – and into somebody else's.[6]

It's a simple idea but it can be transformative because it makes you realise that the problems you're obsessing over barely register to those around you. And so, just maybe, they might not matter quite as much as you think they do.

FIND POSITIVITY

Imagine that you have just reached the summit of Mount Everest. You've finished taking the obligatory 'Look at me! I'm at the top of the world!' photo and have turned around to begin your descent.

This is arguably the most dangerous moment in your climb: the point when you are most likely to lose discipline and start fantasising about being back in your warm bed with a cup of tea. But even though you're trying to take extra care, nothing can suppress your good mood.

And then you arrive at the summit camp, where you had stopped the previous night on the way to the top and left your extra oxygen supplies. And you discover that your canisters have disappeared. They have been stolen.

How would you respond? By throwing a tantrum? Immediately beginning a hunt for the thief? Looking to repeat the crime and steal someone else's supply instead? Or would you find a way to see the positive?

This is not an abstract thought experiment, but the experience of the adventurer Nims Purja, one of the most remarkable people we have met on the podcast. Described by one journalist as the living embodiment of the Blackadder quote 'he laughs in the face of fear and tweaks the nose of terror', Purja was one of our most effervescent guests – a man whose every word fizzed with excitement about the life he's lived.[7]

A former Gurkha and member of the UK Special Forces, Purja has spent much of the last decade climbing mountains the way others might take their dog for a walk – with a cheery smile and a spring in his step. But these aren't just any old mountains. In 2020, he climbed the tallest fourteen mountains in the world, in record time. The previous record had been set in 2013 by the South Korean Kim Chang-ho, who took seven years, ten months and six days. Purja cheerfully passed through the fourteen 'death zones' – such high altitudes that breathing is a struggle and mortal errors highly likely – in just over six months.[8]

This was only the most recent in a long line of astonishing feats. Purja grew up in Nepal, continually on the edge of poverty. 'We came from a really poor family,' Purja explained in one interview. 'As a kid, I didn't even have flip-flops.'[9] But his older brothers too were Gurkas, and they sent home just enough money for Purja to go to boarding school.

It was there that the young Purja first realised that he was unusually resilient. He quickly discovered that he was incredibly fit for his age and excelled at athletics. And he combined this with a fierce commitment to self-improvement, including some rudimentary techniques to enhance these natural talents. 'I would wake up at one in the morning and go out running with metal rods in my socks,' he told us.

His path to athletic greatness was set. First, he too became a Gurka. And then, six years later, he passed the selection for the highly elite SBS. His colleagues in the Gurkhas doubted his capability, having grown up in a landlocked country. 'They didn't know me,' he said. 'I wanted to be in the SBS, because the British Special Forces are the best in the world – 100 per cent, in all respects, on all levels.'

Having ticked off two astonishing feats before his twenty-fifth birthday, it's perhaps no surprise that Purja set his sights on another one: climbing the world's tallest mountain. Despite growing up in Nepal, he had never seen – let alone climbed – Mount Everest. But once he'd had the idea, he couldn't shake it – and, he soon learned, he had an unusual gift for mountaineering. At an artificial altitude training centre he was told that he had a bizarre ability to survive atop mountains: 'my freakish physiology', as he once described it.[10] He did not find altitude difficult in the way that almost everybody else did naturally.

And that's how Purja found himself just a few miles from the top of Everest in 2017, trying to break a world record to climb Everest, Lhotse and Makalu – the first, fourth and fifth highest mountains in the world – and discovering that someone had made off with his oxygen canisters. 'This. Is. A. Crime.' Purja said the words slowly, lest we misunderstand the seriousness of the allegation. 'If your oxygen is not there, it could kill you.'

Purja is not just a master athlete; he's also a master storyteller. So by this point in the conversation, his two interviewers were bristling with indignation. 'How did you respond?' we asked.

His answer was no less remarkable than the incident itself. 'Many people will just get angry and they will blame other people,' Purja said. Indeed, these were his own initial thoughts.

But then he realised something else: that thinking in this way wasn't going to help. If he started obsessing over who had stolen his oxygen, the only person who would miss out was him. He'd lose his focus. He'd feel angry. And those emotions might make him burn through his remaining oxygen even faster.

And so he decided he needed to find a more positive story. 'Come on. Come on!' he demanded of himself. 'There must be something.' Eventually, he came up with a solution. He decided to believe that the thief had been another, less skilled and less experienced climber who was panicking. 'What I said to myself was that my oxygen was used for an emergency situation,' he told us. 'Someone is alive because it was used for their rescue.'

This reframing had an instant effect on his mood – and in turn, his performance. 'I was now happy with the idea that somebody is alive because of me,' he said. These positive emotions allowed Purja to put the incident to one side and begin to think about how he could get down the mountain safely and continue his record-breaking achievements. 'I know now that it could be a complete lie. But then that's the positive message I had,' he said. It was his own small way of keeping his spirit positive.

'It could be a complete lie. But that's the positive message I had.' Nims Purja

Purja's method offers a masterclass in the second way we can respond when we encounter setbacks. All too often, our brains instinctively seek out the worst possible explanation for

131

any given turn of events. *My oxygen tank has been stolen! Nobody likes me! All is lost!*

Sometimes, this might be true. In other cases, not. But every time, telling yourself the worst possible story is rarely likely to help your performance – particularly when you're in the messiness of the Fight stage.

And that's why Purja's method is so powerful: it allows us to find a more positive story – one that helps us fight through the setbacks.

These sorts of cognitive reappraisals are among the many interests of one of the greatest psychologists in history: the Nobel Prize-winning behavioural economist Daniel Kahneman. To Kahneman, the human mind is both a marvel and alarmingly fallible. The Israeli psychologist has spent the past five decades investigating people's automatic thought processes and summarised his findings in his bestselling book, *Thinking, Fast and Slow*. In it, he explained that we have two ways of processing information. For the most part, our emotional, instinctive, 'fast' mind (System 1) runs the show. And it usually works. But when it goes unchecked by our more dispassionate, analytical, 'slow' mind (System 2), we are prone to dramatic errors of judgement.

In particular, System 1 leads us to respond impulsively and emotionally to unpleasant experiences. We create a simplistic story that is based on the most immediate emotions – and not the ones that are most rational or beneficial. As Kahneman summarises things: 'It is easier to fit everything you know into a coherent pattern when you know little.'[11] Consider Purja's words about how most people respond to setbacks: 'People get angry and look to blame others,' he said. *Someone has deliberately stolen my oxygen. Someone wants to harm me.*

But in these moments, we can force ourselves to stop – and to see if there is a more positive story to be told. That involves turning on our System 2 and asking some simple, reasonable questions. *Why would anyone choose to deliberately steal your oxygen? Is there a more benign explanation for what has happened?*

Understanding these two systems helped save Purja's life. He was able to avoid System 1 going into overdrive – and use System 2 to reframe his precarious situation in a more positive light. One day, this method might just save your life too. When things go wrong, force yourself to stop, think and ask yourself some questions. *Is there another, more optimistic story to be told about this setback? How might we see the positive in this situation?*

PITSTOP - HOLE-DIGGING

Humans are great hole-diggers. Spadeload 1: we decide we have a problem. Spadeload 2: we seek out more and more evidence for it. Spadeload 3: we conclude it's completely insurmountable. Before we know it, we've dug ourselves into a problem that's six-foot deep.

It can be helpful to demonstrate to yourself how easy it is to convince yourself you have an issue – and how you can, in turn, think your way out of it. For this one, you'll need to find a partner. One of you should think of an issue (a mild one, mind – nothing too intense) while the other interviews them about it. Ask the following questions in the following order. As you go, the responder should write down their answers.

Question set A

Rate where you currently are on a scale of 1–10.

What is the problem?

Why are you not at 10?

How long have you had this problem?

Where does the fault lie?

Who's to blame the most?

What's your worst experience of it?

Why haven't you solved it?

How do you feel? Mildly devastated about the scale of the issue you face, perhaps? This time, try repeating the interview – but using the following questions:

Question set B

Rate where you currently are on a scale of 1–10.

What do you want instead of the problem?

How will you know you've got this?

What else will improve as a result?

What resources do you already have to help?

Is there something similar you've achieved?

What's the first step?

What effect did asking these positive, solution-oriented questions have on your mood? Did the problem feel that little bit more solvable than the first time around?

We are all world-class when it comes to stressing ourselves out. But with a little positive framing, those stresses can be overcome.

RECALL SUCCESS

When we prepared to meet our first Hollywood superstar guest on the podcast, we expected he would appear from behind a phalanx of PRs, publicists and agents, there to vet our questions and proffer a long list of subjects that were off limits.

Instead, when Matthew McConaughey joined us over Zoom, he came alone – affable, amenable and ready to share his own lessons on *High Performance*. It was the demeanour of a man who had long since worked out how to face the problems life threw at him head-on.

During his childhood in Texas, McConaughey had watched his parents marry three times and divorce each other twice – all while he progressed through school and on to university to pursue a career as a lawyer. It was during this tumultuous childhood that he realised it was helpful to chronicle his life, thoughts and feelings in journals. This process would eventually lead to his remarkable memoir *Greenlights*, which he described as 'thirty-five years of realising, remembering, recognising and gathering and jotting down how to be more me and finding consistent ways that allow me to approach life and get more satisfaction'.[12]

During our chat – which took place late in the evening for us thanks to the differences in the time zones – McConaughey kept referring back to how this deep bank of information about his past helped inform the decisions he made: allowing him repeatedly to swivel in different directions while still acting in line with his own values and beliefs. Every time he was unsure of himself, he had a well of information about his past choices to draw upon.

In particular, McConaughey told us about how he escaped the professional slump that defined the middle of his career – the sort of slump from which most actors would struggle to return. McConaughey, the *New Yorker* once wrote, spent 'a decade in the romantic-comedy trenches in unchallenging movies buttered with cliché'. These years were defined by a series of high-paying, low-demanding roles, such as *Sahara*, *Fool's Gold* and *The Wedding Planner*, the magazine said.[13]

McConaughey didn't like it. 'What I noticed was that being so identified as this was not bringing me other opportunities or other things that I am and want to do,' he admitted in one interview.[14] So, we wondered, how did he reframe this situation to be able to continue his career on the trajectory he wanted?

His answer was to be found in those journals. 'When things are going well, we don't pay attention to what we are doing and why. Only in the dark moments, when things are not going our way, do we appreciate the light. You need to be able to go back and look at what your strengths are and how you can get back to playing them,' he told us. 'Unless you do this, you keep stepping in shit.'

McConaughey was describing a simple – if counterintuitive – approach that we can easily apply when things are going wrong. Seek out past successes and see what they tell you about the problem you face today. Successful examples from your past can become a successful model for your future.

This is an approach that has increasing amounts of scientific backing – not least from a new branch of psychotherapy known as 'solutions-focused therapy'. In classical psychotherapy, you and your therapist will explore your problems in great detail, looking for the roots of your behaviour now – something that might take hundreds of sessions, thousands of pounds, and countless conversations about your relationship with your mother. But, as the authors Dan and Chip Heath explained in their excellent book *Switch*, for half a century we've known of an alternative approach.[15] One which has a surprising amount in common with Matthew McConaughey's.[16]

Starting in the late 1970s, the therapists Steve de Shazer and Insoo Kim Berg noticed that their clients would often speak about their problems without being able to recognise or even acknowledge that not only did they have the inner resources to overcome them, they had also overcome similar issues in the past. As a result, de Shazer and Berg suggest drawing on your past to find solutions for the future.

After listening to a client explain their problem, a solution-focused therapist will ask them to rate where they are on a scale of ten: nought being deeply unhappy and ten indicating perfect contentment. Whatever answer is offered, the second technique employed is the same: ask what the psychologist

Linda Metcalf calls 'the miracle question': 'Imagine when you are sleeping, a miracle happens and all the troubles that brought you here are resolved. Your world is now a ten. When you wake up in the morning, what's the first small sign that would make you think, *Well, something must have happened – the problem is gone?*' Then comes the final, all-important question. *When was the last time you saw some evidence that this miracle has come true?*

This final ask is one of the most powerful tools in a therapist's kit. It shows that this 'solution' is already present in people's lives in some form or another. Because it proves that the client already has the resources to overcome this setback. If the problem has been solved before, it can be solved again.[17]

This method – of focusing on your past to gain a new perspective on your future – would help transform McConaughey's career. He told us that he often looked back through his own history – all those journals – when he felt he was losing a sense of connection with his career to remind him of what he most loved about acting. And that analysis of his past led him to a dramatic decision: to step away from Hollywood and refuse the romantic comedy roles in which he had found himself typecast. 'I went away for a while, and I didn't know how long I'd have to be away when I stopped doing romcoms. No one was offering me the roles I wanted,' he later explained.[18]

It took nearly two years – and an iron-like resolve to turn down a $14.5 million offer for a romantic comedy role – before offers that played to his actual interests started to come in. 'Being gone, not seeing me shirtless on the beach, not seeing me in your living room, or in a romcom, I became a new good idea,' he once joked. 'Where's McConaughey been? We forgot about him.'[19]

His screen return, which he dubbed 'the McConaissance', was validated in 2014 when he won his first Oscar for his performance in *Dallas Buyers Club* – a role in which he lost 45 lbs to play a straight man diagnosed with Aids who becomes a kingpin distributor of unapproved HIV remedies. Not exactly a romcom, then.

McConaughey's method offers the final, revolutionary way to thrive in the face of setbacks. When things go wrong, the instinct is to conclude not only that you can't solve them – but that *nobody* has ever solved them. It's impossible, you tell yourself as you give up on your dream.

But the truth is, in most cases, we have already solved these problems. Look at your history. You have already changed careers. You have already rebuilt your relationships. You have already learned new skills.

You have already achieved the impossible, then. By looking to your past, you remind yourself of all the fights you've already won. And that empowers you to spring energetically back into the ring.

LESSON SUMMARY

*Is there a way to see the setbacks you face
not as problems but as opportunities?*

- When faced with setbacks, it's easy to become fatalistic – to conclude that this problem isn't just for now; it's *for ever*. But there's another way. We can learn to reframe the problems we face so we see they are minor, surmountable – and won't determine the outcome of our change journey.
- How can we see our problems in this light? First, by getting a sense of perspective. When we're in our own heads, we struggle to see our problems clearly – but by getting an outsider's take, we can often understand what's really going on.
- Second, by seeking out the positive in even the most irritating news. There's a bright side to every situation – it just takes a little discipline to find it.
- Finally, by seeking out past successes – and reminding ourselves that we have overcome similar setbacks before. Most setbacks are nothing new. Ask yourself, *How did you bounce back last time?*

Climb

Don't just change today. Change for ever.

Change isn't about moments. It's about systems.

FROM ACTIONS TO SYSTEMS

'The best never get bored with the basics.'

One of the most influential rugby coaches in history was sitting before us, explaining the secrets of high performance. With his distinctive and gentle lilt – the voice of a man raised in Yorkshire who had spent most of his adult life in Scotland – Ian McGeechan was describing how he had created a culture of excellence in a succession of triumphant teams: Northampton, London Wasps and, most famously, the British and Irish Lions.[1]

We had imagined that he was going to unveil some sweeping, revelatory theory of cultural change. We thought wrong. 'I've called it world-class basics,' McGeechan told us. It was just as simple as it sounded.

'Each position or each role has certain skills that are very specific to that role,' McGeechan explained. 'The best are able to deliver something that can make a difference when it matters.' These small, basic skills – consistently passing the ball well, consistently converting a try – add up to elite performance.

'The best are able to deliver something that can make a difference when it matters.' Ian McGeechan

Is that it, we thought? Could the difference between average and high performance really be the skills that, by McGeechan's own admission, were the most low level? But he was adamant. As an example, he cited a famous moment in the British and Irish Lions' 1997 victory over the Springboks. It was an iconic moment, in which the outside centre Jeremy Guscott landed an unexpected drop goal in the closing moments of the second Test match – taking the Lions to an 18–15 victory and an uncatchable 2–0 series lead. And yet, McGeechan emphasised, none of the players was doing anything particularly special. One player won a line-out. Another ran a hard line and was tackled. Another passed to Guscott. And Guscott kicked the winning drop goal.

World-class. And basic as anything.

McGeechan's outlook teaches us something important about the next stage of your change journey. So far in this book, we've explored how to identify a new life for yourself and leap into it. We've talked about the setbacks you'll encounter and how to overcome them. We've come a long way.

But we've still only explored how to change your life in the short term. And that's what Step IV is all about. Its lesson: Don't just change today. Change for ever.

In the climb stage of your change journey, you need to find a way to embed the changes you've made. You need to create systems that allow you to perform with consistency. You need to find a way to execute the basics right every time, just like the Lions do.

Lasting change isn't about moments. It's about systems. And such systems are the focus of Lesson 7. In the pages that follow, we're going to explore how to create systems that embed change into your behaviour in the long run.

For if you really do learn to turn your behaviour into an endlessly repeatable method, your change journey will be nearly complete. As Bruce Lee observed: 'I fear not the man who has practised 10,000 kicks once, but I fear the man who has practised one kick 10,000 times.' This lesson will teach you what effective practice – effective change – actually looks like.

IMMEDIATE GOALS

The first way we can turn one-off behaviours into consistent systems comes from the remarkable life of Ash Dykes.[2]

Growing up in North Wales, Dykes was not your typical adventurer. He had neither a military background nor a wealthy family to fund his expeditions. He simply sees himself as 'a passionate traveller who loves seeing new places and setting himself increasingly difficult challenges'.

This is perhaps something of an understatement. By the age of twenty-five, the self-taught explorer had two world records to his name – the first for trekking across Mongolia and the second for crossing Madagascar. When we met him, he had recently returned from walking the full length of the Yangtze river in Asia, a feat which took him across 4,000 miles over 352 days to complete.

'It had it all,' he smiled, casually talking us through his adventures like others show holiday snaps. 'There were rapids and tributaries I had to cross; mountains too. There was some amazing wildlife, such as wolves. And even Asian giant hornets. If they sting you, it sets off a pheromone that causes the rest of them to target you. It only takes a few of those stings to kill you.

'They kill over fifty adults a year,' he concluded breezily. 'In total, it was around eight million steps I had to take.'

If we weren't paying attention when Dykes mentioned the murderous giant insects, his matter-of-fact reference to those eight million steps certainly made us sit up. How on earth had he done it?

We soon learned that his method was simple but visionary. He chose to focus not on the end goal – which would always be alarmingly distant – but on his short-term objective.

During his first record-breaking hike across the Gobi Desert and Mongolian Steppe, Dykes decided to break the whole trip down into day-long tasks. 'My dad taught me to break the goals down, majorly,' he explained. 'I got the map out and looked at every single one of those days. It was anticipated to take about a hundred days and so I looked at every single possible day.'

This had a transformative impact on his mindset. 'When I broke it down like that, I realised that every day was possible. As long as I had the right food supply and hit the right water points, there was nothing major enough to stop me from achieving it. Breaking the goals down helped manage my expectations,' he said. 'If I hadn't, the task would have seemed so overwhelming, I would have changed my mind.'

This approach is what got Dykes through the hardest – and most dangerous – parts of his expedition. One day, he inadvertently missed one of the water refill points on his journey. 'I was suffering with dehydration and heatstroke, which can often prove fatal in those conditions,' he told us. 'I had no shelter, no breeze, wild visions and relentless headaches. The only option for me to survive was to get up and keep walking.' The next water source was four days' walk through the desert.

So what did he do, we asked? The answer, he said, was to stop feeling 'sorry for himself' and instead focus on breaking the four days into tiny, manageable steps. 'I couldn't visualise four days but I could visualise a hundred metres. I would break my goals into 100 metres. I would walk for 100, maybe 200 metres and then rest under the trailer, sometimes for an hour,' he told us. 'Although it was slow and painful, I was making progress; I was getting closer. By staying disciplined I just about made it to that community where I had shelter and water.'

This focus on the process is the most effective way to turn one-off changes into long term habits; individual moments of excellence into world-class basics. 'Don't rush the process,' Dykes said. 'Just enjoy the moment, stay in the moment, take your time and still pace it out day by day. You're going to get there.'

'Don't rush the process. Just enjoy the moment.' Ash Dykes

The science is clear: Dykes' approach works. In their brilliant book *The Progress Principle*, business analysts Teresa Amabile and Steven Kramer explored the idea of focusing on these so-called micro-objectives when they studied 12,000 diary entries from 238 people to get a picture of the subjects' inner work life.[3] A common trait of highly successful people is the relentless focus on achieving 'small wins': tiny, incremental victories that alone don't seem like much but which add up, over time.

This is just what Dykes was doing in the Gobi Desert – and it's just what we should do if we want to build long-term behaviour change. Don't focus on the end goal; focus on the short-term objective. The ultimate objective will take care of itself.

CONTINUAL FEEDBACK

Ben Francis can remember the precise moment he experienced 'ego death'.

It had been nine years since he had founded Gymshark as a teenager with his friend from school, Lewis Morgan (who we met in Lesson 1). It had been eight years since a friend had taught him to screen-print the first Gymshark T-shirts. And it had been just a year since Gymshark's exponential growth had turned it into one of Britain's few 'unicorns' – that is, a private company worth over a billion dollars.[4]

So it was understandable that Francis thought he was pretty good at his job. In 2017, he had stepped down as CEO in order to learn how to lead a company of such size, scope and significance – instead becoming chief marketing officer as well as the de facto public face of the company. Now, it was the summer of 2021 and he was feeling confident as he returned to the role of CEO.

His first step: undertaking a 360-degree feedback exercise from his colleagues. The results weren't pretty.

Francis described the process to us. 'You list people around you that you work with or spend a lot of time with, and they describe you and add in comments. I had eight people contribute to it.' But the results were much more vicious than he had expected. They told him he was too abrasive, too direct, and lacking in empathy. 'When I read it, it completely broke my heart. I thought, *That's not me*,' he told us. 'That just doesn't sound like me. Everyone else is wrong.'

It was the chance intervention of his wife that made Francis take the note seriously. He took the feedback document home and absent-mindedly left it on the kitchen table – where his wife Robin found it. 'I was so annoyed that she'd read it,' he told us. 'But she said: "That's the most accurate description of you I've ever seen."' In that moment, Francis told us, time stopped. 'It was a really, really important moment.'

From then on, Francis found himself becoming more open to criticism. While his first reaction was to dismiss the feedback as wrong, he quickly let go of his ego and accepted his peers' sincere and valuable insight. No longer burdened by the need to project an infallible image, he was free to move forward. It was transformative for the business, he said. Once he had taken responsibility for what he describes as his 'reinvention', it was a natural progression to plan his self-improvement. And it worked; at the time of writing, the company is in the middle of an aggressive expansion into the US – and is worth a third more than it was when Francis returned as CEO.

Francis's ego death (and partial ego recovery) hints at the second way to turn your one-off behaviours into long-term systems. When you are in the middle of your change journey – as Francis was in 2021 – it is easy to stop taking feedback. You get complacent because you're so far into your journey. You need to find a way to continue to improve.

To do so, it can be helpful to create a feedback system – one that means you are continually being prompted to transform your behaviour. Such systems involve receiving sharp, specific, personalised feedback about what isn't working – so you can continue to embed the changes you seek every day.

But what do effective feedback systems look like? My favourite explanation comes from the work of the executive coach Marshall Goldsmith, whose books *Triggers* is a must-read for anyone interested in how to create reliable systems of behaviour change.[5] He gives the example of a driver heading down a road approaching a village, who spots a sign that says 'Speed Zone Ahead 30mph'. The data, alarmingly, indicates that at this point, most people don't bother slowing down – it's only a sign, after all, and they're still thirty seconds away. After half a minute you arrive in the village, where the sign has a more absolute quality: it says 'Speed Limit 30mph'. At this point, most drivers slow down a bit – but not enough to actually get to 30mph, which suddenly feels like a distant prospect.

This is a little like Francis at the helm of Gymshark. He was doing things the way he had always done them. And gentle, generic prompts to change weren't enough to actually do so.

So what can be done? Well, consider an alternative prompt for our speeding driver. Goldsmith highlights the remarkable power of *interactive* speed signs – that is, a digital sign that says 'Your speed', followed by a number. Surprisingly, when drivers see these signs they slow down with astonishing consistency: compliance increases by between 30 and 60 per cent when they are in use.

According to Goldsmith, these signs work because they are a form of 'feedback loop'. As he puts it, they 'measure a driver's action (that is, speeding) and relay the information to the driver in real time, inducing the driver to react.' Action. Information. Reaction. And best of all, at the end of the process it starts again – because the little dopamine hit you get from seeing your lower speed lit up in green is a prompt to repeat the behaviour again. The result: people actually respond to these signs when they'd ignore any other.

This three-part mechanism is a little like Ben Francis's experience of behaviour change. There was a clear, specific action: the prompt of the feedback process. He received information about his actions, which was specific and relatable to his own experience. And he reacted: which led to better productivity of his team – which began the feedback process anew.

Fortunately, such feedback systems can be integrated into our lives with relative ease. The trick is simple: ask for it. Talk to the people around you and ask them questions like, *What could I be doing differently? How could I be improving? What is going wrong, and what is going right?*

Even better, try to integrate this culture of feedback into your average year – scheduling feedback from your colleagues, your friends, and even your family every few months. What has gone well in the last few months? What could I have done differently?

Before long, you'll find that your behavioural improvement becomes self-sustaining. You won't slip or get complacent about your world-class basics. You'll be undergoing a process of continual change.

PITSTOP - SIX STAGES OF FEEDBACK

We're all capable of listening to about 600 words a minute. Unfortunately, we're only capable of speaking about 150 words a minute. That means we process feedback much more quickly than people express it.

As a result, our brains have usually run off in twenty different directions before the person giving us feedback has finished. And that can be a problem: we don't take in the right information and instead draw our own – often deranged – conclusions.

That's why it can be helpful to break down the stages we experience when we receive negative feedback. There are six of them: *Shock. Anger. Denial. Rationalisation. Acceptance. Action.*[6] And we can divide them into two parts. *Shock, anger* and *denial* are all part of the emotional response – what the psychiatrist Dr Ceri Evans calls 'the red zone'.[7] *Rationalisation, acceptance* and *action* are about coming to terms with the feedback in a constructive and considered manner – which Evans called 'the blue zone'.

Unfortunately, we're often stuck deep in the red zone by the time the person who's giving us feedback has finished. But there are ways to progress through the stages in a more rational manner. Think through some recent feedback you received – and in the 'experience' column, reflect on how long it took you to process it. How do you think you process feedback? Do you tend to get stuck in the red zone – and if so, how have you got out of it before?

Stage	Emotion	Experience
The red zone	Shock	
	Anger	
	Denial	
The blue zone	Rationalisation	
	Acceptance	
	Action	

VISUALISE SUCCESS

In 1965, the pioneering social psychologist Howard Leventhal concocted an experiment to research what might convince a group of Yale University students to get vaccinated for tetanus.[8]

He asked each student to read a booklet describing the effects of tetanus and the benefits of inoculation. But there was a difference between the seemingly similar-looking booklets. Some were given a 'high fear' version, which described the illness in alarming detail (replete with pictures). Others received the 'low fear' version, in which the language was vague and not particularly worrying.

Leventhal hypothesised that the 'high fear' version would prompt higher levels of inoculation than the 'low fear' one. It made sense: after all, one of the groups of students had just been given a horrific photo of somebody having a tetanus seizure. They would care more, right?

Wrong. In his seminal book *The Tipping Point*, Malcolm Gladwell explains how nothing about this experiment unfolded as its designers anticipated. For a start, *neither* group seemed to respond to the information in the booklets. Sure enough, the 'high fear' version led the students to *say* they were going to get inoculated. The trouble was, they didn't actually go through with the jab. As the blogger Sam Thomas Davies summarises it: 'One month after the experiment, almost none of the students had actually gone to the health centre: only a mere 3 per cent had got inoculated.'

It was an interesting insight. Fear wasn't enough. And so Leventhal changed tack.

He decided to redo his experiment – with one small but significant change. This time, for one group, he included a map with the site where you could get a jab circled and gave prompts on specific times they might go. The results were astonishing. This time, 28 per cent actually went and got inoculated – across both groups of participants.

Why was fear so unsuccessful in motivating a behaviour – but a specific prompt of a time and place was? The answer relates to the way we think about our own behaviour. When we *visualise* an action, we're much more likely to do it. The key was turning the abstract concept – 'Going and getting a tetanus jab . . . ' – into a visual representation image – '. . . at 9 o'clock at the university hospital on the West side of the campus'.

Since Leventhal's pioneering study, dozens of experiments have shown that this process – visualising the changes we want to make – is key to embedding behaviour change for good. If you want to commit to your behaviours in the long term, you need to learn to picture them in your mind. When you do, you get a clearer vision of where you are going – one that is possible to truly commit to.

This helpful principle might just explain the recent resurgence in interest in the phenomenon of 'manifesting'. We, your authors, have been on something of a journey on this. We confess that, when we first encountered the work of Roxie Nafousi – the author of *Manifest* – we were a bit sceptical.[9] The whole thing sounded a bit woo-woo.

But then Nafousi told us her story and we realised she might be on to something. 'At the age of twenty-eight, I'd never known happiness,' she said at the beginning of the episode.

'My life was just a complete blur of hedonism, parties, come-downs, depression, anxiety and low self-worth.'

Her worst moment came after a two-week yoga retreat in Thailand, which she had hoped would lead to a change in her life. 'On my first night back home, I got invited to a dinner, did a line of cocaine and stayed up for forty-eight hours. I remember lying in my bed, staring at the walls, trying to sleep and thinking, *I fucking hate myself*,' she said. 'If 200 hours of meditation and yoga are not going to change me, what is the point in life?'

In desperation, she called a friend, who suggested she explore the idea of 'manifesting'. Eventually, the method would change her life. 'My life began to change from there,' she said. 'Not all of a sudden, but the journey to where I am today began.'

And what a change it has been. Today, Roxie Nafousi is a world-renowned manifestation expert, podcast host and best-selling author who has worked with an enviable client list that includes celebrities such as Kourtney Kardashian to help them understand how manifesting can work.

Manifesting is, according to Nafousi, nothing more than 'the ability to use the power of your mind to change and create the reality you experience'. The trick is all about clearly imagining the world you want – and reaching for it. But it's not easy. 'A lot of people think manifesting is about sitting, waiting and wishing. Or they think that you can just think really positive thoughts and then the things you want will appear in your life,' Nafousi told us. 'But manifesting is not a passive process. It is, in fact, quite the opposite. It requires action. It requires you to step outside your comfort zone, take risks, align your behaviour and act as your future self would.'

'Take risks, align your behaviour and act as your future self would.'
Roxie Nafousi

Above all, the trick is to create a clear image of the world you want. The first step in Nafousi's manifesting guidebook is the simplest: 'be clear in your vision'. Sketch it out if you like: create 'a visual representation of what you want your life to look like in one year from now'. But in every case, try to make it as specific and vivid as possible. 'Be really conscious of when you're restricting yourself from asking for the things you want and instead, force yourself to dream bigger,' she says.

Whether you believe in manifesting or not, Nafousi's method hints at how visualising change can help us embed it into our behaviour. As Leventhal's study shows, visualising an action makes us much more likely to actually do it; Nafousi's method is a more spiritually minded equivalent of the map showing students where to get their tetanus jabs.

We can all use this method in our day-to-day lives. When you're deep into your change journey, it can feel difficult to remember where you've been – let alone where you're going.

That's where visualisation comes in most handy. When you feel yourself getting complacent, stop. Visualise another world. And reflect on what you would need to do to make it real. By imagining a different future, you go a long way towards creating it.

LESSON SUMMARY

*How can you turn this one-off positive action
into a lifelong positive behaviour?*

- You've reached the Climb stage and the end of
  your journey is in sight. But you're not there yet.
  You need to find a way to turn individual positive
  actions into reliable, consistent habits. You need to
  create a behaviour change *system*.
- In practice, this involves three simple steps. First,
  break your desired behaviour down into small,
  manageable steps. 'Change your behaviour for life'
  is hard to digest. 'Change your behaviour today' is
  much easier.
- Next, see if you can look for continual feedback
  from your surroundings. Could you ask your
  friends, team-mates, or even family to offer you
  continuous advice on how you're changing (and
  how you're not)?
- Last, try to visualise what success would look like –
  and live up to that vision wherever possible. Once
  you've imagined changing your life – and really
  thought about what that means – it becomes much
  easier to make it real.

You can go further than you think.

THE FINAL STRAIGHT

The end of the marathon might not be the hardest part. But it might just be the most dangerous.

While most runners know about the 'wall' – the moment, usually around mile twenty, when you feel you simply cannot go any further – fewer know about its relative, the 'X-spot'. This is the point 26.1 miles into a 26.2-mile race where runners turn the corner and see the end in sight. The psychologist Shawn Achor describes it as 'the point the brain releases a flood of endorphins and other feel-good chemicals that carry the athletes through the final minutes of the race and euphorically over the finish line.'[1]

If they're lucky, anyway. Sometimes, the excitement of arrival is literally enough to kill people off. The X-spot is, remarkably, the place in the entire marathon where you are most likely to experience a heart attack. This is why so many major marathons have medics set up right next to the finish line. At the 2011 Philadelphia marathon alone, ten people needed resuscitation at the X-spot.

One need not be a marathon runner to have experienced the perils of the very final stage of a journey. The finish line is a dangerous moment. Kenton Cool, the British climber who has scaled Everest sixteen times, explained on the podcast that the moment you can see the summit is one of the most difficult moments a mountaineer can face. It is so tantalisingly close that you relax and the chances of mistakes increase. Something similar was suggested by Kelly Holmes, who famously won gold in the 2004 Athens Olympics 800-metre race by just 0.05 seconds. She told us that only by maintaining your focus until the very end of the race can you be sure of success.

These final moments of your change journey are the focus of Lesson 8. The home straight is euphoric. But it is also the most exhausted you'll ever be. You might let your guard down. Or take stupid risks.

In these moments, it helps to remember that you can go further than you think. You just need a strategy. One that helps you maintain your energy right up until the final moments. One that allows you to power through the X-spot and barrel down the home straight.

GET A DEADLINE

The cover of AJ Tracey's eponymous debut album shows him looking bored, staring into the middle distance while cradling a baby goat. The image symbolises his self-anointed status as the GOAT: greatest of all time.

So when Tracey came on the podcast to discuss his meteoric rise to become one of Britain's most highly regarded rappers, we weren't anticipating humility. Yet in truth, Tracey was as chatty and relaxed as guests come – and more than happy to talk us through his weaknesses as well as his strengths.

'I'm secretly lazy,' he told us. 'If I can achieve something without doing the maximum effort, I'll do it.' This is not something that you would guess from Tracey's glistening CV. His rapid-fire vocals, which move effortlessly between grime, trap and drill, have brought him astonishing success. Tracey's first album – the one with the goat – was the second biggest selling album by an independent artist in 2019. And he's done it all without signing to a major record label. 'This allows me to do whatever the hell I want,' he explains.

Tracey – real name Ché Wolton Grant (named after the Argentinian revolutionary, Ché Guevara) – began his ascent to the summit of the world's most competitive industry at the age of thirteen, when he began uploading music to SoundCloud. Even then, he had prodigious talent. Tracey puts his creativity and rapping skills down to his Welsh mother, whom he reveres. A former pirate radio DJ, she introduced him to a wide, eclectic range of music – from dancehall to rap, garage to jungle – all in their home on a council estate in North Kensington, west London. His Trinidadian father, meanwhile, taught him how to write lyrics, having been in a UK hip-hop group in the nineties. Most importantly, according to Tracey in one newspaper interview, he taught him to rap about 'the dilemmas of being black, which my mum can't teach me'.[2]

Social inequality formed the focus of much of Tracey's early music. 'I was very angry: angry at society, angry at life, angry at everything,' Tracey once said. 'That's how I was feeling, so all my music sounded very aggressive, violent, angry, all these negative things.'[3] And it hit the mark: Tracey's music was soon being played across London. The buzz was getting louder by the month.

There was just one problem. Even as his profile grew, Tracey was nervous about dropping everything to focus on music. Always serious about studying, he had enrolled for a criminology degree at London Metropolitan University. 'I was unsure whether I could get people to listen to my rap,' he explained to us. And that left him uncertain about which path to take.

That's where Tracey's mum stepped in. 'She said: "If you wanna give this a shot, I'll give you a year."' She told him to take twelve months off studying or worrying about earning money and focus solely on kick-starting his music career. 'The mental effect was powerful,' Tracey told us. 'It was a blessing. I thought: *My mum's giving me a golden opportunity. I can't squander my time here. I have a year, so I have to make it work within a year or this is pretty much done because I don't have any money.*'

Today, Tracey credits the deadline his mother gave him for launching his career. It gave him the final burst of energy he needed to commit properly to his music. And it hints at the first way we can propel ourselves over the finish line of our change journey.

Deadlines are weirdly powerful, particularly when you're at the end of an arduous task. When the finish line is in sight – whether that's releasing your first EP or merely getting a new job – we can get complacent. Deadlines offer discipline. They focus our minds – and they motivate us to keep speeding along the final straight.

This is not just an anecdotal observation. Dozens of psychological experiments over several decades have shown that deadlines can transform our behaviour. Consider the research of Nira Liberman, a psychologist at the University of Tel Aviv. In one experiment, Liberman asked a group of students to undertake an arduously dull task – completing 240 computer-based tasks that required a high level of concentration, which between them would take about ninety minutes. But not every undergraduate got the same treatment. Some were constantly told how close they were to the finish line – the others were not given any information about how far through they were.

Liberman found that the students who knew they were close to the end were much more successful – and also felt less fatigued once the task was complete. She also noticed that they showed signs of an 'end spurt' – they knew how close they were to finishing, and it made them speed up as the deadline loomed. They knew the deadline – and it convinced them to focus.[4]

We can see the effects of this process in AJ Tracey's career. When he recorded a particularly good song during his twelve-month trial period, he told us, he wasted absolutely no time getting it out into the world. 'I released a song on SoundCloud, which was good,' he says. But he knew there was no time to waste. He had soon taken to googling every opinion-forming music broadcaster he could find. 'I searched the names and then found their emails and bombarded them with my track,' he said, laughing. 'I'm quite well spoken so I introduced myself well.'

And this wasn't just a few dozen broadcasters. 'I sat down and I compiled over a hundred different emails of people I've never met or heard of,' he said. 'They don't know me. I just believed, surely one of these people is like a taste-maker.'

He was right. Sian Anderson, a presenter from BBC Radio 1Xtra, heard it and recognised Tracey's rare talent. 'When she said this is a good song, it doubled up my confidence,' Tracey says. Anderson began playing his song. Other radio stations soon followed.

'Never get stuck in a moment.'

AJ Tracey

Tracey still credits that moment – and his mum's deadline – with helping him achieve lasting success. He says it shows the power of continuing to look forward, even as you reach the end of your journey. 'I've shown you can do what you want, how you want, and there's still room for you,' he says. 'You should never get stuck in a moment.'

PITSTOP - THREE GOALS

Dame Kelly Holmes knows a thing or two about speeding across the finish line. Her performance in the 800 metres at the 2004 Athens Olympics is one of the most iconic finishes in modern athletics history – the famous day she won gold at a point in her career when many had concluded her best days were behind her.

When we met Holmes on the podcast, we were interested in how she kept herself focused through her training and right up to the finish line of the race. Her answer related to the three discrete types of goal, each of which kept a different part of her mind focused.

First, there were *outcome goals*. In 2004, the outcome she sought was a gold medal in the Olympic 800-metre

---

final. 'I have dreamed for ever to be the best at what I do,' she wrote around that time. 'Some dreams come true, but my biggest ones are still out there and I really want them to become reality.'[5] The gold medal was the big, ambitious outcome that kept Holmes motivated.

But while this goal was compellingly bold, it didn't tell Holmes much about her actual behaviour. That's where her *performance goal* came in. With her coach, Holmes analysed her previous results, her opposition and her own capabilities – all to conclude that a time of one minute and fifty-eight seconds should be enough to win the race.

Finally, Holmes needed a way to focus on *how* she was going to train and run. And so she finally identified three *process goals*: remaining calm, ensuring that she stayed out of the pack, and practising her final 'kick' in the home straight.

These three goals gave Holmes the vision, the knowledge and the behaviours she needed to sustain her performance to the very end of her journey. And it's a method we can all use. Come up with a goal you're striving for and then divide it up into three more immediate goals: outcome, performance and process goals. *How will you use them to propel yourself over the finish line?*

My overall goal: _____

_____

_____

_____

My outcome goal: _____

_____

_____

_____

My performance goal: _____

_____

_____

_____

My process goal: _____

_____

_____

_____

THINK POSITIVE

Imagine you are exhaustedly plodding towards the end of a marathon when you hear a shout from the sidelines: 'Hey, you fucking asshole. I'm not cheering for you. I saw how slow you were on the last split. When you cross the finish line, I'll give you a polite clap. Now fuck off.'

These were the memorable words of Mel Robbins, one of the world's most influential writers on motivation, when she came on the *High Performance* podcast. But she was not actually just screaming abuse at her interviewers (we think, anyway). Robbins was highlighting that while we would – hopefully – never speak to other people in such abusive terms, we frequently berate ourselves in a similarly unhelpful manner. This negative inner-voice often does us far more harm than good – and we're particularly likely to fall victim to it at the very end of a hard journey, when we're tired and fed up.[6]

But how can we tackle these voices? Fortunately for us, Robbins is an internationally bestselling author renowned for her work on the simple, devastatingly effective actions that can help us achieve our true potential. In particular, her focus is on how *acting* happy can, in turn, make us *feel* happy. Her key suggestion: start your day with a high five. To yourself. In the bathroom mirror.

This was an idea that stretched the credulity of your two authors, it must be said. 'Can we be honest and admit we are a little cynical about this?' we offered as our opening contribution to the discussion. Mel's response was instant and scathing.

'Don't do it, then,' she retorted. 'How is cynicism working for you? Like, what have you got to lose? Seriously, what if this is actually the secret? Like, how hard is it, honestly, to stand in your knickers in front of a bathroom mirror and raise your hand?'

The effects were profound. 'I saw a profound shift in my happiness, mood and energy from doing this high five habit – and it wasn't just me,' she said in one interview. 'I posted a photo of myself doing it online, with no explanation, and soon, thousands of people were writing to me, sharing that they were also high-fiving themselves, and seeing massive changes in their attitude and confidence.'[7]

Why does the self high five work so well? Robbins pointed us towards a surprisingly wide array of research that holds the answers. She told us, for example, about a study from the University of California, Berkeley into NBA basketball players. At the beginning of a season, researchers recorded how often players gave each other high fives and other signs of encouragement like fist bumps and back slaps. They were able to predict which teams did better – and which worse – based on the number of high fives per match.[8]

'The best NBA teams – those who made it to the championships – were the ones who consistently gave the most high fives at the start of the season,' she writes in her book.[9] 'It comes down to trust. The teams who high-fived constantly lifted each other up,' Robbins told us. 'It helps you shake off a bad play. It lifts your mood. It communicates confidence. A high five reminds you that you can still win.'

'A high five reminds you that you can still win.' Mel Robbins

Robbins' method hints at a second way to maintain motivation at the end of a race. Have you ever found that, at the end of an arduous task – whether it's a long, difficult meeting or the run-up to a fiendish exam – you find yourself utterly exhausted? In turn, you might start thinking negative thoughts. *I can't do it. I'm too tired to continue. I may as well give up.*

With hindsight, you can usually see that the end was closer than you thought. So you need to find a way to lift your spirits – and keep going over that finish line.

In these moments, think of Mel Robbins' example. Embrace positivity and act in a way that is as positive as you want to feel. Give yourself a high five in the mirror. And keep going.

DON'T STRUGGLE

'I have an elder half-sister, and I made her cry once playing Monopoly.'

Johanna Konta was describing the years before she became one of the world's best tennis players. She had always had a competitive streak. 'I didn't have many friends when I was younger,' she told us. 'I think because I was competitive ... Everything was a race.'[10]

This sense of competition had a powerful effect on Konta. From the first time she picked up a racket in Sydney, Australia, it was love at first sight. She had soon decided: she wanted to be one of the very best players of her generation. That ambition would take her around the world – first to the Sánchez-Casal tennis academy in Barcelona at the age of fourteen, and then to Britain, where her parents moved with her in her late adolescence, ultimately becoming British citizens in 2012.

But for all the sacrifices Konta's family made to support her ambitions, Konta's early professional career was relatively unremarkable. Everyone could see she was technically brilliant. But her attitude was less so. She developed a reputation for suffering on-court meltdowns when faced with pressure situations, and she didn't threaten the world's top 100 for the first four years. Her desire to always win was no longer helping her advance; it was holding her back.

And yet by the time we met Konta in 2022, her reputation had transformed. Over the previous decade, she had reached grand slam semi-finals at the Australian Open, French Open and Wimbledon, and won the Miami Open. Widely acknowledged as Britain's best female tennis player of her age group, Konta peaked at world number four in 2017.

How did she turn things around? She credits this remarkable second act of her career to the psychologist Juan Coto. Her results quickly improved – particularly because, as she says, Coto helped her get better at controlling her emotions. In particular, he taught her to cut herself some slack.

Konta described to us how she became overinvested in a series of unconscious ideals about how the world *should* be. *I should win today; I should be doing better; I shouldn't make mistakes.* When the world wasn't like that, she would beat herself up – sometimes very publicly. She explained to us the voices echoing around her head when things didn't go according to plan. 'I was trying to force things and would get quickly frustrated when they didn't happen. *This isn't fair! This isn't how it's supposed to go. Why is this happening to me?*'

In their sessions, the Spanish psychologist helped Konta to recognise this unhelpful habit – and began setting some ground rules for her own thinking, which in turn would relieve some of the stress these demands were causing. Coto outlined a simple formula to understand this way of thinking:

Struggle x Resistance = Pain

'He explained to me that there would always be moments when things went wrong,' she told us. 'The key was how I was responding. If the struggle was a ten and I fought it by losing focus or blaming others, which was also a ten, the pain was a hundred. However, if I stopped resisting and accepted those moments as part of the journey – in other words, reduced it to zero – the pain would become zero.'

 'There would always be moments when things went wrong. The key was how I was responding.' Johanna Konta

Konta credits this idea with transforming her approach to tennis. She found that writing small reminders on her equipment, including simple affirmations such as 'enjoy it', 'look up' and 'smile', helped to keep bringing her mind back to the moment. She was able to stop struggling in moments of discomfort and, instead, learn to embrace them – and then get on with the game and her day.

To us, this reveals the final way to maintain momentum at the end of your change journey. These final moments are not only the most tiring; they are also the moments when we are hardest on ourselves. Have you ever found yourself indulging in the thoughts that Konta identified: *I should do well today; I should be doing better; I shouldn't make mistakes?*

In these moments, it can be helpful to stop, rest and cut yourself some slack. The race is hard enough. You don't need to make it worse by being hard on yourself. So stop struggling and try to enjoy the process.

That, at least, was what Konta learned. 'Juan was a tremendous influence on me,' she said of her mentor, who died in 2016. 'It was about more than just tennis – it's about my life in general and my happiness as a person.' Her coach had helped Konta get over the finish line to a new life.

LESSON SUMMARY

*How will you maintain your momentum along
the final straight and over the finish line?*

- The most dangerous part of any journey is the end.
  This is when we get complacent and make stupid
  mistakes – ones that could jeopardise our whole
  transformation. But it doesn't have to be this risky.
- We can stop ourselves from giving up on the final
  straight with the help of deadlines. Give yourself a
  hard end point for your project. And stick to it.
- We can sustain our momentum along the final
  straight with a little positive thinking. Remember
  Mel Robbins' self high five? What is your version
  of waking up every day and giving yourself a high
  five in the mirror?
- We can eliminate negative self-talk on the final
  straight by cutting ourselves some slack. You've
  come so far, and you might be tired. But the worst
  thing you could do is talk yourself down. So give
  yourself a break – and remind yourself that the end
  is closer than you think.

Arrive

Change is not a noun. It's a verb.

Arrival is about more than just arriving. It's about all the journeys ahead.

YOUR NEXT ADVENTURE

When Ben Francis stepped down as CEO of Gym-shark, he had already led the start-up through a period of astonishing growth, pioneering the use of online influencers to sell clothes and, in the process, turning an enterprise he launched in his parents' garage into a million-pound brand. Many thought he'd never lead the company again. They thought wrong. In 2021, Francis returned as CEO – this time at the helm of a company two orders of magnitude bigger.

When Mel Marshall announced she was retiring from swimming, many thought her best days were behind her. She had, after all, shattered the British 200 metres freestyle record four years previously, and been ranked as the best swimmer in the world. How could she possibly top that? The answer came when she turned her hand to coaching. Within a few years, she was the force behind the record-smashing success of Adam Peaty – largely responsible for his astonishing string of golds at major championships including the Olympic Games.

And when Alex Scott stepped back from professional football, her career was festooned with stunning highs: the second-most-capped player in the history of England's women's team, she had represented her country at three World Cup tournaments. Some footballers might be tempted to leave it there. Not so, Scott. Just months later, she was back on television screens – this time as one of the lead football presenters on the BBC.

Many of the people featured in this book are chameleons. Their early careers were defined by astonishing achievements in sport, business and the arts. They went as far as they could. They took some time off. And then they came back transformed – as the world's great broadcasters, writers or coaches. They changed not once, but many times.

These change-makers are our inspiration in Step V. To get here, you've come a long way, so take a moment to congratulate yourself. You've dreamed of a new life, you've taken the first leap into the unknown, you've fought your way through the obstacles, you've climbed to the summit (or, at least, you've read a book about how you will). And now you've arrived. How does it feel?

But there's more. Because arrival is about more than just arriving. It's about all the journeys ahead.

If there's one thing we've learned from our interviews, it's that the most remarkable people are never content with changing just once. Like Francis, Marshall and Scott, they have undergone many changes. They know that change never ends, whether we like it or not. And so it falls to us to keep changing in the ways that we change.

Change is not a noun. It's a verb: a process that will continue, whether you like it or not. So once you've arrived at your destination, you might find yourself asking: *What next?* This lesson is about just that. Our focus: how you can turn change from a one-off journey – with a beginning, a middle, and an end – to a process of never-ending improvement.

ESCAPE COMPLACENCY

How can we ensure we're changing for the better not just once but for ever? As good an answer as any comes from one of the most chameleonic guests we've hosted on the podcast: Gary Lineker.

When we sat down opposite Britain's greatest player-turned-TV presenter, we were keen to understand the lessons we might glean from his incredible career. Or rather, his two careers: the first, his journey to become the talismanic captain of the England football team; the second, when he transferred 'from the box on to the box' to anchor *Match of the Day*, eventually becoming one of the country's favourite sports broadcasters. It has been a process of perpetual metamorphosis.

'I've been very lucky,' he told us repeatedly. But it was more than luck, as we suspected. His success was thanks to the distinctive approach he took to the process of self-improvement. In particular, his knack for placing himself in places in which he was continually challenged and could never become complacent.

This idea cropped up again and again throughout Lineker's interview. He told us that, throughout his career, he was blessed to be surrounded by people who refused to let him stop improving – whether they were parents, coaches or fellow players.

At the beginning of Lineker's career, this encouragement

took a rather unorthodox form. Born in Leicester, Lineker's natural talent for goal-scoring gave him the opportunity to leave school and join his home club Leicester City – he first played for the youth team in 1976. His first manager, Jock Wallace, had an old-school approach to fending off complacency. 'I was starting to make a bit of progress and we had a reserve game,' Lineker told us. 'He came in at half-time, cursing away. "You fucking useless little . . ." he said – and I then realised he was looking at me! He picked me up by the scruff of the neck, threw me against the dressing-room wall and said: "See me in the morning in my office at 9."'

After a sleepless night, Lineker reported to his manager's office at the designated time. 'I was a gibbering wreck,' Lineker said. 'I sat outside like a naughty boy waiting to see the headmaster. I was trembling as I thought I was going to be shown the door.' But when he was summoned, Wallace had a surprise in store for the young striker. '"You were magnificent last night,"' Wallace said. '"I just wanted to make a wee point, that you've always gotta give a little bit more. Let that be a lesson in life."'

What was the effect of this feedback, we asked? 'I thought, *My God. Wow*,' Lineker said. 'I also thought: *You could have told me last night*.'

Now, to be clear: this book is not in favour of throwing teenagers at walls (most certainly not when they're Gary Lineker). But Lineker did emphasise that this lesson stayed with him. You must never get complacent – and you must always be seeking out your next challenge, even when you're performing well.

In time, Lineker would thankfully find a coach with a more sophisticated way of overcoming that complacency – Terry

Venables at FC Barcelona. For much of his early career, Lineker had been coasting. He had become known as a good but not exceptional player, whose potential was seen to outstrip his performance. He also had an unhealthy reputation for being unwilling to put the hours in. 'He was a terrible trainer,' Harry Redknapp once said. 'He just liked to come in on Saturday and play.'[1] Lineker admitted as much on the podcast. 'I don't think I was the hardest worker in the room in terms of training,' he said. 'I'd do it but I didn't really enjoy training because I didn't think it ever was that helpful. I wanted to practise what I do on the pitch.'

And yet after a lackadaisical start to his career, Lineker had an astonishing second wind in his late twenties. He scored his first international goal at the age of twenty-four. And he never looked back. Three years after playing in the Second Division with Leicester, he was signed by Barcelona. In 1986, he scored scored six goals for England at the World Cup, to win the Golden Boot for the tournament's top scorer. By the end of his career, he had scored forty-eight goals for his country.

How does Lineker account for this transformation in his fortunes? He puts it down to the coaching style at Barcelona, which eradicated any sense of complacency he might have felt. 'I used to get really kind of frustrated by how training used to be,' Lineker told us. 'What I wanted to do was practise my craft, which was making runs, scoring goals, and getting into dangerous areas. Whereas most of the training was always a disappointment. It used to bore me. It didn't stimulate me.'

This boredom at training began to change when he arrived at a team that knew how to *really* challenge him. Head coach Terry Venables had moved to Barcelona a couple of years before Lineker, taking the Catalan club to its first title in eleven years. Venables had enjoyed a celebrated playing career before establishing a reputation as an exciting, innovative coach. He understood that the key to helping Lineker succeed was to get him out of the same old training routines – all that drilling and monotonous practice – and force him to think differently.

To do so, he came up with a peculiar strategy: invite Lineker to lunch. 'I used to think a lot about the game and under Terry, most of my best training took place off the training ground,' Lineker told us. 'We used to go to lunch two or three times a week and we'd just discuss football and movement. I played for lots of really good coaches but his coaching was so different.'

As a result, Lineker found himself being challenged – *really* challenged – for the first time in his career. It involved deep thought about what would work, which he could then experiment with on the pitch. 'Terry would come to me with ideas and we would talk about it and then we'd try them,' Lineker recalled. 'I loved that. Thinking about the game made me better. I enjoyed thinking about how to get better.'

'I enjoyed thinking about how to get better.' Gary Lineker

Why did Venables' strategy help get the best out of Lineker when his previous coaches hadn't? The answer lies in a nineteenth-century fairy tale. Most people know the tale of Goldilocks and the Three Bears. You'll recall how Goldilocks liked the porridge that was neither too hot nor too cold, but 'just right'.

As it turns out, this is a useful way for sparking continual improvement. A century after the famous Goldilocks story was first published, the psychologist Lev Vygotsky offered a more academic exploration of this same effect.[2] Vygotsky's point was that it is unhelpful to throw a person incapable of swimming into the deep end of a pool; just as it is to have an Olympic swimmer paddle around in the baby pool and seriously expect them to improve. The ideal zone for practice is in areas where a task is appropriately challenging: what he called the 'zone of proximal development'.

The Goldilocks zone – the area of proximal development – is the place where we are at our least complacent, and most able to continuously learn. As Robert Bjork, the chair of psychology at UCLA, explained it in an interview with the writer Daniel Coyle, 'There's an optimal gap between what you know and what you're trying to do. When you find that sweet spot, learning takes off.'[3]

This is what Lineker got at Barcelona: just the right level of challenge to keep on getting better and better. 'I wasn't the best footballer,' Lineker said with characteristic humility. 'But I was the best goal-scorer for two or three years.'

There's a powerful insight here for anyone who wants to continually improve. Whatever change we've talked you through in this book, there will probably come a point where it starts to feel easy – whether that takes a week, a month or a year. Eventually, you'll feel comfortable in your new life. You might start to slow down.

This is a risky moment; the point where you're most likely to get complacent. The solution? Ask what the 'Goldilocks zone' would look like for you. What would it mean to seek out the next challenge? Go for the next promotion? Take up a new handicraft? Seek out new friends?

Change is perpetual. When you reach every destination, you will spot a new one on the horizon. Seek out the people and places that encourage you to walk straight on towards it.

PITSTOP - QWERTY THINKING

Have you ever wondered why your computer keyboard begins at the top left with the letters QWERTY?

They aren't, after all, the catchiest of letters. Nor the most frequently used. Nor the start of the alphabet. Indeed, QWERTY is probably the most inefficient series of letters you could pick. And that's the point. In the earliest days of typewriter design, typing too quickly would cause the keys to stick. So engineers needed a way to slow people's typing down – and they duly came up with the most confusing design possible. (It was also to help sell typewriters: the letters that spell the word TYPEWRITER are all on the top line, which was helpful to typewriter salesmen if less so to the rest of us.)

Fast-forward 100 years and we have no such sticky-keys issue (and most typewriter salesmen are out of a job). But we're still stuck with the QWERTY layout. Where we started determined where we ended up.

This is a lot like the way people stop changing. They embark on a particular route and get stuck on it. If you want to tackle complacency and continue to transform yourself through life, you need to escape QWERTY thinking.

The following tools have been designed to help you generate new ideas about where to go next – by

---

breaking away from the restrictions imposed by your own past. Consider the following as you brainstorm your next challenge. What new ideas will escaping QWERTY thinking bring?

1. **Suspend judgement.** When we're coming up with ideas, it's tempting to shoot down any half-baked suggestions the moment they're expressed. Resist. When you're trying to escape QWERTY thinking, an open, free-wheeling creativity is what you're looking for. There's no such thing as a bad idea.

2. **Seek understanding.** When you've stumbled upon an idea that feels good, try to look at it from many angles. Simply asking questions such as 'why?' and 'how?' of yourself will help you scope it out. Only stop asking these questions when you feel you have a deep understanding of the idea's strengths and weaknesses.

3. **Build it out.** Once a preliminary idea has passed through these two stages, try to build it into something more concrete. *What would it mean to add additional components to the idea before you? What is the broadest application of this idea that you can think of?*

JUMP RIVERS

As we stood backstage at Salford's Lowry theatre, we watched our guest limbering up with irrepressible energy. We could tell already that we were in for an interesting interview.

One of Britain's leading stand-up comedians and TV

presenters, Russell Kane came across as a whirligig of excitement, his searing humour leaving our live audience helpless with laughter. One newspaper critic described him as 'a comedy David Attenborough who, instead of the animal kingdom, focuses his attention on the way blokes from the south-east behave'.[4]

Growing up in Essex, he was a bookish wallflower in a world of geezers. 'I was a weedy boy at school and my dad was hyper-masculine, steroid-using, weightlifting, meat-eating 16-stone nut job,' Kane told one interviewer.[5] His interest in reading provoked hostility and suspicion rather than encouragement, especially from his father. But it did help him achieve a first-class degree followed by a career in advertising.[6]

In his early twenties, two life-changing moments arrived within a month. His father died. And he performed his first-ever stand-up gig.

'I'd gone home for Sunday lunch and said: "I've done something crazy. I'm going to do an amateur comedy night. It's in the diary at the end of September." My dad didn't look up but said: "I tried it once. Waste of fucking time."' Deflated, Kane left. And, tragically, his dad died unexpectedly on holiday soon afterwards. It was the only comment on Kane's stand-up that his dad ever made.

The event led to deep reflection from Kane on his relationship with his father. His dad could never bring himself to tell his son how proud he was of his son's achievements, Kane told us. The only time he saw his father show any emotion was when his favourite Indian restaurant shut down. 'I found his diary after he had died,' Kane said. 'It was really sad; the most bleak thing I've ever read. It was one to two words every day.

Rained. Work was shit. Bad traffic. Wow. It was like the haikus of an Essex man on a downer.'

Kane resolved in that moment that his life wasn't going to be like his dad's. 'I've spent a lot of time trying to work out who I am,' he said. 'I don't fit with my family or the people in my estate.' And sure enough, his life wasn't like his dad's. Kane's relentless work ethic and innovative approach to comedy set him on a trajectory to the top of his field. In 2010, he won the best comedy show at the Edinburgh Comedy Awards, and since then, his career has been a whirlwind of endless change – from presenting BBC shows, to writing a novel to, always, touring new performances.

We were interested in how Kane had continued to shapeshift throughout his career. He began his answer by giving us an account of his own career to date. Your comedy career, Kane said, can launch in one of two ways. In the first, you take off and never really come down. 'This is the one you want,' he said. The other is trickier. 'The second – which I got – is a brilliant take-off, in which you go up' – he pointed to the ceiling – 'you get about five years' work, then you need the next jump that leads into a more long-term, sustainable career.'

So how do you leap from the first change to the second one? Kane's answer relates to self-awareness. 'My numbers [for tours and bookings] never dropped, but they began to flatten off,' he explained. 'I knew there was an issue because I was doing the most television and radio I'd ever done.'

Kane was quick to spot his error, even if it led to a bruised ego. The spotlight had made him lose his authenticity, he said. 'The exposure goes to your head. The content of my shows changed. I started talking about being a stand-up comic in my stand-up routines. How unrelatable is that? I developed this bizarre haircut with a streak in it.' In short: he had lost his relatability. 'When you are in my business, you must have authenticity.'

Today, Kane is scathing about the Kane of ten years ago. 'Talking about my dad and mum, my nan and doing funny things about my family whilst wearing leopard skin trousers and eyeliner created a disconnect,' he says. 'People couldn't relate to me as a working-class man.'

So what did Kane do? He made some big changes. 'I changed management. I grew up with my look, and I stopped doing slightly immature things like lying about my age.' He also changed *that* haircut. 'I've been really strict about making sure my hair's combed,' he has said.[7]

Kane describes this process – of leaping from one life step to the next – as 'river jumping'. 'It was something I came across when I worked in advertising,' he said. According to the advertising executive Dave Allan, co-author of *What If?*, river jumping is a process of looking at a situation in a completely fresh way, by moving from the stream you're in – whether that's your job, your relationships, your hobbies – to a completely different one. As they put it, you need 'to get out of the original river altogether, then approach it from a new and different perspective'.[8]

Kane offered us some advice on how to do so. 'Instead of trying to find a solution for your craft, look at a totally separate industry and go, what would they do? So, for example, if you're a rock climber, ask what would a boxer do? It might just provoke something.' It's a method that has a knack for unlocking creativity (a favourite fact of Damian's: roll-on deodorant was created by looking at the ballpoint pen and the similarity where a liquid had to be spread equally thinly across a surface). And it gives you an entirely different perspective on your job and your life.

 'Look at a totally separate industry and go, what would they do?' Russell Kane

The river jumper's approach changed how Kane approached his own career; he forced himself to look at his stand-up-oriented stand-up routine and his nifty haircut from a stranger's perspective – and concluded he looked like 'a pretentious attention-seeking penis' (his words, not ours).

But you do not need to be a penis to use this method. All it takes is looking at your situation afresh. When you've arrived at your destination, ask yourself: *What would my life look like if I were someone else entirely – a stranger I met on the street, my three-year-old child, a member of a remote Amazonian tribe?* Think about your life from an entirely different viewpoint. Drop all preconceptions, past experiences and prior knowledge about the problem. And see what you find.

In this moment, you start to see your change journey from a wholly new angle. You are not somebody at the end of a long, arduous journey – ready for a lie-down and a nap. You are somebody at the beginning of your next transformation. Someone for whom the change journey is always just beginning.

LESSON SUMMARY

Now that you've arrived, what next?

- High performers are never content with changing just once. Change is eternal. So how can we ensure we're continually transforming – not just now, but for ever?
- The first step to continuing your change journey is simple: escape complacency. Seek out environments in which you're constantly challenged – and in which the community around you continually forces you to get better.
- And the second step is even simpler: 'jump rivers'. *What would it look like to take another life-changing leap – into a better career, a better worldview, a better life?*

Leadership isn't a title. It's a mindset.

LESSON 10

PASS IT ON

John McAvoy has lived a life of two halves. The defining feature of the first one: crime.

His introduction to London's criminal underworld began young. When he was an eight-year-old growing up in south London, McAvoy had been given a criminal 'apprenticeship' by his stepfather, Billy Tobin. Tobin's own life had been defined by trauma, including being forced to witness the murder of his father at knifepoint. It lit within him a determination to always retain control; never be a victim. By the time he appeared in the young boy's life, he had already served just over half of a sixteen-year sentence for armed robbery.

'Look at all these people,' Tobin once told McAvoy, as he pointed towards London commuters trudging into work from the comfort of his latest car, a brand new Porsche. 'All these people out there are sheep.'[1] Tobin was beginning an education process that taught McAvoy that working and paying taxes would never lead him along the path to success. He had to go another way.

Just before Christmas in 1993, Tobin took his protégé to an Italian restaurant to meet some criminal acquaintances. They greeted the young man warmly and generously. 'I took home nearly a grand in cash, which is not bad when you are ten,' McAvoy recalled in his spellbinding autobiography. And from there, he never looked back. He went to jail for the first time at the age of just eighteen, but it made little discernible impact – if anything, it made him even more sure of the life he had chosen. 'A lot of the people I was surrounded by had already been to prison,' he said in one interview. 'I learned that it was all about not showing weakness and fighting it. So that's what I did.'[2]

And yet by the time we met McAvoy, he was a different man. A Nike-sponsored athlete, he is one of Britain's leading Ironman champions – and a multi-record-holding rower. He spends his days advocating for the power of sport to turn people's lives around. And he's lost none of his spark. 'I once had a plan on how I was going to buy this place,' he announced to us when we interviewed him at the top of the BT Tower. 'Honestly, I was going to get it.'

What changed? How was a down-and-out criminal able to become one of Britain's most respected sportsmen? The answer hints at the final lesson in this book – one that relates to how change is always a collective endeavour.

You see, we've spent the first nine lessons in this book exploring how you can change your own life, individually. How to Dream of a different world and Leap into it. How to Fight through the obstacles and Climb to the summit. We've shown you how to change *yourself*.

But as we'll see, McAvoy's story shows another side of change: the way that each of us can change *others*. And in our opinion, that is the final ingredient in learning to change. From changing yourself to learning how to pass it forward.

This is arguably even more important than learning to change yourself. You're not in this world alone. If you want to build a community in which everyone can excel – be that in your sports team, your workplace, or even your family – you need to learn to influence others. You need to become a leader.

We know, we know – 'leader' is a daunting word. But the fact is, leadership is something any of us can achieve – and we tend to have more power than we think. As the late entrepreneur Dame Anita Roddick once said: 'If you think that you are too small to make a difference, try going to bed with a mosquito in your room.'

Her point was that leadership isn't a title, it's a mindset. Any of us can effect change in our communities, starting today.

How? That's the question this lesson will answer. We'll see how the example of John McAvoy's life offers us a simple three-step framework for changing the lives of the people around you – one that the acclaimed writer Alan Deutschman (a huge inspiration for this book) first identified in his seminal work *Change or Die*.[3]

Deutschman wrote that all three steps hinge on the power of positive relationships. All three, memorably enough, begin with 'R'. And all three offer a way to move from transforming your own life to transforming those of your peers. To move from merely changing to being a change-*maker*.

RELATE

The beginning of John McAvoy's change journey began in September 2005. The 22-year-old McAvoy had agreed to raid a security van in south-east London along with one of his old associates, Kevin Brown. Unbeknown to McAvoy, there was a detailed surveillance operation in place waiting for Brown to commit an offence. McAvoy's involvement was regarded as a welcome bonus.

As soon as the pair moved to hijack the security van, the police swooped in and started pursuing them both. McAvoy was chased through a housing estate and ended up face-down and trapped. 'I had about fifteen guns pointing at me as I lay in the road of a little cul-de-sac,' he once said. 'I was absolutely deflated.'[4]

Their mood was in stark contrast to the jubilation felt among the arresting police officers. 'They put me in the back of this undercover car and the same police officer who'd arrested me the very first time was gently calling my name,' McAvoy once told an interviewer. 'He said to me: "John, look out of the window." There were people out on the high street with their shopping bags. "You will not be seeing this for a long time," he said.'[5]

This time around, McAvoy's reputation preceded him. 'The powers-that-be thought me to be such a high escape risk that they deemed me a threat to national security,' he laughs. He was placed in one of the most secure prisons in the UK, a place the authorities were so keen to be impenetrable that they once tasked the SAS with trying to break out (they couldn't). McAvoy found himself surrounded by a who's who of the criminal underworld. 'I recognised all the notorious faces from the newspapers,' McAvoy says. '[The convicted terrorist] Abu Hamza comes up to me, really polite, and says: "You've just been arrested, haven't you? Do you need anything?" I said no, I'm absolutely fine, thank you.'[6]

After a protracted trial, McAvoy confessed his guilt and was eventually sentenced to fifteen years in that prison, a decision he described as 'like watching your life being hit by a train'. In that moment, McAvoy couldn't have known that this time prison was going to be different – that this time he was going to leave a changed man.

The first few years were the same as ever. McAvoy sat in his cell doing nothing much. But in his third year, he changed things up – and started to attend the prison gym. Once there, he chanced upon a friendship that would change him for good.

Darren Davis, one of the prison guards and a keen amateur athlete, spotted McAvoy's athletic potential when he took part in a fitness competition. They made an unlikely pair. 'I had no respect for people like Darren at all,' McAvoy told us. 'He was my captor. I hated him.' But Davis was undeterred. He resolved to keep offering McAvoy words of quiet encouragement. And soon, McAvoy started to notice its effects. 'For the first time in my whole life, I had a male in my life that genuinely cared for me and wanted me to be successful just for the sake of me being successful,' McAvoy told us. 'He had no vested interest. There was no contracts, no money, no nothing.'

As the months turned into years, the bond between the men grew. 'I had never trusted anyone in authority,' he said, 'but Darren was the first person in that position who truly believed in and encouraged me.'

This burgeoning relationship hints at our first 'R': 'relate'. According to Alan Deutschman, this is the point when you 'form a new, emotional relationship with a person or community that inspires and sustains hope'. You connect with someone, and that gives you the best possible base to change their thinking.[7] Why? Because by building a relationship with someone, you can start to transform their self-perception. You plant the idea in their heads that they can do better.

Indeed, the science is increasingly clear that strong relationships aren't just the best way to effect change in others – they are the *only* way. For a long time, behavioural scientists thought that the primary motivator of human behaviour was punishments and rewards – a worldview known as 'behaviourism'. But more recent studies have concluded that, in fact, behaviour change is rooted in strong relationships. John Bowlby, the pioneer of 'attachment theory', has shown that the way we form relationships – most notably the attachments we form with our parents from birth to the age of three, but also throughout our lives – is the determining factor behind how we learn, change and grow.[8] Our relationships make us who we are.

And when we think about it, most of us realise we have already experienced the power of relationships in changing our behaviour first-hand. Have you ever had a teacher who you felt really believed in you? Or a boss who seemed to desperately want you to be your best? Or perhaps a mentor a few years older in school who seemed genuinely invested in your success? If so, you've experienced the power of the first 'R'. These figures didn't just help you *believe* that you could change – they emphasised that they *expected* you to do so. And so change you did.

This is precisely what Darren Davis offered to McAvoy. He built a real, loving, personal connection with McAvoy – and used it to inspire him. '"Mate, if you don't change your ways, it will be the greatest waste of potential I have ever seen,"' McAvoy recalled him saying.[9]

'Those words had a massive impact,' McAvoy told us. They were words that he had never allowed anyone he respected to utter before.

PITSTOP – BIDDING WAR

The psychologist John Gottman views conversations as a series of 'bids'. In this context, a bid is not quite something you'd place in an auction or poker table – it's merely any expression that invites a response. And usually we don't even notice we are making them.

When you're trying to build a relationship with someone, positive 'bids' are one of the most powerful tools in your arsenal. In his studies of marriages in the 1980s, Gottman concluded that people's bidding approach can make or break a relationship – even though, at first glance, the differences between them seemed tiny.[10]

So, what are the most common types of bids? In their book, *Mind Gym*, the authors Sebastian Bailey and Octavius Black invite us to imagine the following scenario.[11] Your partner is sitting in front of the television, watching their favourite programme. You enter the room and ask whether they fancy a cup of tea. Your partner now has the chance to respond in one of three ways:

1. **The 'toward bid'.** They respond in a *positive* way. 'Yes please – strong with lots of sugar.'
2. **The 'against bid'.** They respond in a *negative* way. 'Ugh, no – your tea is gross.'
3. **The 'away bid'.** They just stay silent or change the subject. 'What are we doing this weekend?'

The research indicates that using plenty of 'toward' bids has a huge positive effect on relationships. In fact, the magic ratio for a healthy, lasting relationship seems to be 5:1 positive ('toward') to negative ('against').

This is a helpful insight for platonic and workplace relationships, too. When you're trying to relate to a person you'd like to influence, think about the bids you're using. *What bidding style are you most prone to? What is your ratio of toward to against? And how might adopting a more positive style strengthen the bonds you're trying to forge?*

REFRAME

McAvoy's family name brought him plenty of respect in the prison community. So he enjoyed perks that other criminals could only dream of – including access to contraband items. Chief among them was a mobile phone.

On the evening of 14 November 2009, he was on his prison bunk idly watching a football match on television when he received a phone call from his cousin Bill. He would deliver two words that would completely change McAvoy's outlook.

'Mate,' he said softly. 'I've got something to tell you. *Aaron's gone.*'

Aaron Cloud had been McAvoy's best friend and partner in crime – a man he had grown up alongside, lived beside, and had an inseparable bond with. Cloud had promised his friend that somehow he would help him escape from prison. But it wasn't to be. He had been thrown from his car while trying to escape from a robbery he had committed in the Netherlands, and died from a broken neck.

The news had a devastating impact on McAvoy. 'I was utterly shattered,' he recalled. 'I'd never lost anyone I cared for and then suddenly my best friend dies.'[12] McAvoy spent days 'seesawing between anger and grief'. But as he started to recover from the shock, he was offered a tool that gave him a starkly different perspective.

'The prison chaplain came to see me,' McAvoy says. 'I used to be quite dismissive of him in prison. I never used to really engage. But he came to my cell and he sat down on the bed. I told him how unfair life is. "My friend did a bad thing, but he was a good person and now he's lost his life at twenty-six years old."' The chaplain listened and offered a consoling – and soothing – thought. *You were blessed that you had him in your life, and had that interaction with him while he was alive.*[13]

It was a subtle shift in mindset that would offer McAvoy the next tool he needed to change his life. The prison chaplain's words taught McAvoy the second of our 'R' words: 'reframe'. This is the point in which 'the new relationship helps you learn new ways of thinking about your situation and your life'.[14] Here, the chaplain was reconceptualising the problem

McAvoy faced – and demonstrating that there was a less bitter and painful way to think about it.

We've already encountered the power of reframing in this book; it is the key tool we used to view our own problems clearly, way back in Lesson 1. But when we teach *other* people to reframe their problems, it offers them even more than it can offer us when we do it ourselves. Because not only are we helping them understand their issues clearly – we are also reassuring them that we care about them too.

It was an inspiring approach. And in time, McAvoy began to find ways to reframe his own circumstances – even without the chaplain's help. Influenced by the death of his friend – and inspired by the priest – he began to look at everything differently. 'All the people I'd admired and looked up to since I was a little boy were just old men rotting in prison, and they'd done nothing with their lives,' he found himself realising.[15]

This is what helping people reframe their situation can do. By telling him to focus not on his friend's death but on his own life, the chaplain had awoken a profound shift in mentality. 'It was only then I realised how precious life is,' McAvoy says. 'I got up the next morning and I was completely lost. My reputation, my name – it was all meaningless. I looked at myself in that prison cell and knew I had wasted my life up to that point; down the drain.'[16]

As he came to terms with this new way of seeing the world, he resolved to begin changing his ways. He made a profound decision: 'I am not living this life any more,' he said. The chaplain had inspired him to reframe his situation. And suddenly, the road was open to becoming a different John McAvoy.

REPEAT

From that moment, McAvoy gave himself over to sport. But fortunately, he wasn't starting from scratch – not quite, anyway.

The qualities that had made him successful in the underworld – quick wits, ruthless decision-making and deep levels of concentration – all translated equally well to his physical training. What's more, Darren Davis's relationship and subtle coaching interventions – and the insights into his situation that the chaplain had offered him – helped him recognise this and gave him a renewed determination to excel.

At first, his aim was simply to top the prison's gym leaderboard for various physical challenges. He heeded Davis's advice and discovered that his raw athletic potential translated particularly well on the indoor rowing machine. Davis encouraged him to persevere, even bending the rules to let him train longer than the other men in the gym.

Then he stepped it up a gear. Davis went to the prison governor and gave a testimony about McAvoy's changed character, which allowed him to train for a twenty-four-hour indoor rowing challenge. And so he got training. The results, though, were beyond anyone's wildest imagination. When the challenge came, he broke two world records – one for 100,000 metres and the second for the furthest distance ever rowed in twenty-four hours.

When McAvoy sat in his cell following this achievement, he felt better than at any time he could remember. 'The same way, if not better, than I used to feel coming off a job with £20,000,' he said. For the first time, thanks to Davis's gentle, continual encouragement, he was forced to acknowledge a private truth to himself: 'I was really, really good at something.'

Davis agreed. He kept on emphasising to McAvoy that he had a talent. And this acknowledgement lit a spark within McAvoy. His thirst for knowledge became insatiable. 'Suddenly, I had positive goals and an understanding of the discipline required to achieve them.' He started devouring books on sport and nutrition from the prison library. 'I learned about electrolytes and body fluids; I became conscious of the food I ate; and I learned about how to improve my mental strength. I lapped up everything I could, sometimes reading 500-page books in a weekend.'[17]

This burgeoning knowledge helped him recognise how his characteristics could lead him to a life of success, not just crime. 'A lot of these characteristics that I had – the will to win and want to be successful – I only used to see in criminals and suddenly there's this other group of people,' McAvoy once told the BBC. This other group was made up of athletes. 'The mindset was the same but I just had to channel the energy into something positive.'[18]

This change in mindset – unleashed in large part by Davis's encouragement – offers us our third R: 'repeat'. This is the stage you commit to and embed the change through continual repetition; the point at which 'the new relationship helps you to learn, practise and master new habits and skills that you will need'.[19] It's hard to get a better example of that than Davis: continually praising McAvoy's performance, helping him reach new milestones, and encouraging him when the going got tough.

These little encouragements – particularly when they come

from someone you respect – are life-changing. Like all high-performance leaders, Darren Davis understood that change is all about repetition: continually reminding people of the expectations created by your relationship. Once you get that right, people – like John McAvoy proved – will leap through hoops of flames for you.

It's an insight we can all learn from. If you want to change the people around you, don't just tell them that you believe in them – what you expect of them – as a one-off. Tell them every day. That you believe they can win that race. That you know they can ace that exam. That you're certain they can really secure that promotion. The more you repeat it, the truer it will feel. Lasting change is built on repetition.

Between them, these three 'R's – the moment Davis first related to him, the time the chaplain helped him reframe his life, and the repetition that Davis emphasised in the gym – had set McAvoy on the path to a completely different way of being. They created new connections, new thinking and new skills. They offered him everything.

Towards the end of our interview, McAvoy told us about his first parole hearing after he got into sport for the first time. 'The judge sat across the table from me and said: "What are you going to do when you get released?",' McAvoy remembers.

'I said: "I'm going to become an athlete."'

'With his glasses on the bridge of his nose he looked up at me with a smile and said: "In all my years of sitting in hearings for life-sentence prisoners, you are the only one who has sat in front of me and said that."'[20]

But McAvoy wasn't kidding. When he was finally released from prison in 2012, one of the first things he did – after getting a Nando's and going to see his mum – was to head to the London Rowing Club in Putney. He was determined to make it as a professional rower. And he never looked back. Soon, he had turned his mind to endurance sports and triathlons, eventually landing sponsorship from sports giant Nike and competing in Ironman races. He is a different John McAvoy.

And what does this new McAvoy love to do more than anything? He wants to pass it forward – to inspire others. McAvoy hopes that he can change other people's lives in the way the prison chaplain and guard did his. He once described his mission as helping other people change their situation through the power of sport: 'I am so adamant and so driven that other people get the same opportunity to turn their lives around and find their purpose and direction in life,' he said. 'If I can go through that journey and process of change, it's possible for anyone. I am so determined to help other people get the same chance.'[21]

 'If I can go through that journey and process of change, it's possible for anyone.' John McAvoy

It's this mindset that creates real, permanent change – not at the level of individuals, but at the level of societies. Changing yourself feels good. Changing whole communities is the best feeling in the world.

McAvoy knows that from experience. He understands that when you're in your lowest moments, little interventions from people are one of the only things that can get you out. 'I regret everything I did as a young person,' he told us. 'I've always accepted full responsibility for my actions. No one made me do what I did when I was a young kid and when I was a man. I made those decisions and I do regret them.'

But it taught him something powerful. 'I don't regret spending the time that I spent in prison, those ten years,' he told us. 'It's where I grew as a person. It changed my mindset. It changed my outlook on life.'

LESSON SUMMARY

*How can you help the people around you
change in the way you just have?*

- Now that you've learned to change, it's time to spread it around – to move from being on a change journey to becoming a change-*maker*. How can each of us help the people we meet change their lives, too?
- That process involves three 'R's. First: 'relate'. Good relationships are the foundation of all persuasion. If you can connect with the people you meet, you can start to influence them.
- Second: 'reframe'. Help people see their problems from a different perspective. *How might you encourage them to view their experiences anew?*
- Third: 'repeat'. Repetition is the basis of all lasting change. If you can encourage people to repeat positive behaviours every day and week, you're well on your way to changing not only your life but theirs too.

Change is all you are.

THE NEVER-ENDING JOURNEY

After the chaos of rehearsals and the blizzard of technical checks, there was a moment of calm.

It was the first night of our *High Performance* theatre show, and we were waiting backstage to welcome thousands of guests to spend the evening with us.

'How are you feeling?' one of us asked.

'Nervous. You?'

'Shitting it.'

We laughed the awkward laugh of two men trying – failing – to find levity in a stressful situation. This night was the product of months of preparation and weeks of rehearsals. But more than that, it was the product of a lifetime spent trying to learn from the best about their journey to high performance.

Why were we so nervous, we started to wonder? Well, in the course of our podcast interviews, we learned that fear often wears a disguise. At first glance, we thought we were worried about fluffing our lines, forgetting our links or falling

217

over our feet (all of which we managed to do, incidentally). But the real reason was hidden beneath those concerns: *What if we were just two guys standing in front of a 2,000-person crowd who really didn't have any answers to give?*

We said as much to each other, and the words hung in the air for a moment. They didn't sound great. Then, after a beat, Damian said: 'Well, what if we are?'

In this book, we've tried to sketch out a roadmap to changing your life. We've explored how to Dream of a new life and Leap into it. We've examined how to Fight through the obstacles and Climb to the final summit. We've even touched on how, when you Arrive at the summit, you can begin to think about your next journey.

But that pales into insignificance compared to what we haven't offered. We *haven't* told you exactly which steps you need to take to leave your job, find a new partner, or launch a business. We *haven't* offered you specific lines to use in that tricky conversation with your boss about why you're quitting, to seem charming on a first date, or to explain to your mum why you've just invested all your savings in some utopian new venture. We're not trying to solve your problems outright.

But in the course of this book, we hope we've offered something as useful. We don't have the answers. But hopefully we've helped you ask yourself the right questions. *What would a new life look like for you? Why are these obstacles in your way, and how might you surmount them? How can you create personalised behaviour systems that will help you reach the summit?*

These questions are all we can offer. There's only one person who can change your life. You.

This book offers a roadmap. But you will always be the map reader.

A JOURNEY WITHOUT A DESTINATION

The *High Performance* podcast began in earnest when the two of us and our brilliant producer Finn jumped on a train to Portsmouth to interview the Olympic gold-medal-winning sailor Sir Ben Ainslie. We met on a cold, slate-grey afternoon by the English Channel in a greasy spoon café near the Ineos Team UK boatyard. And as we waited for Ainslie to arrive, we casually speculated on the kind of replies we might expect.

If we're honest, we anticipated that our podcast guests would share their own versions of the Al Pacino speech from the *Any Given Sunday* film. You know the one: when Pacino makes his inspiring speech to a young group of American foot-ballers to 'climb out of Hell, one inch at a time'.

And if we're to remain honest, that's secretly what we wanted.

We loved the idea of hearing about how very *different* these remarkable people were from the rest of us. How they were the ones who didn't buckle under the weight of expectation. The ones who lived through intense sacrifices and stress. The ones who were resilient in a way the rest of us could barely imagine.

Except, that wasn't what we got at all. In every conversa-tion, we've been struck by how *ordinary* these extraordinary people are. How they too have found it hard to change. How they too have struggled with the desire to give in. How they too have had moments of ambivalence about where they're even going, and whether it's even worth it. So what truly separates high performers from the rest of us, we wondered?

The answer, we eventually realised, was simple. These people weren't motivated by the abstract ideal of high performance. They were focused on the joy of the journey.

Because ultimately, the journey is all there is. 'Travel changes you,' the chef Anthony Bourdain once said. 'As you move through this life, you change things slightly, you leave marks behind, however small. And in return, life – and travel – leaves marks on you.'[1] It is these little marks arising from the journey of life that make you 'you'.

As our tens of podcast interviews entered the hundreds, this idea has come to occupy our imaginations more than any other. Early on in our recordings, we adopted Phil Neville's definition of high performance – *doing the best you can, where you are, with what you have*. We stand by it. But more recently, we have come to realise something else: that 'where you are' is not one fixed point.

'Where you are' is changing, constantly. It moves as we grow up. It moves as we take on new challenges. And it moves when we meet new people. You are not just somebody who is changing. Change is all you are.

And that's why change is never about the destination. It is always about the journey.

'Shall we tell them that?' Jake said as we waited in the wings of the auditorium.

'Yes, let's do that.'

And we walked out into the blinding lights of the stage.

ACKNOWLEDGEMENTS

Jake

I want to thank everyone who has opened my eyes to change over the past forty years. And by that, I truly mean everyone. Of course, my amazing parents, incredible wife, wonderful children and great friends, family and colleagues, but not just them.

Thanks to the bullies who forced me to change schools. Thanks to my manager at McDonald's who sacked me for 'lack of communication skills' – true! Thanks to the exam markers who gave me an E, N and U for my A-Levels. Thanks to the hundreds of TV executives who rejected me early in my career.

I'm grateful for everything that has happened, positive and negative, because every experience builds us. The bullies made me resilient, my fast-food boss opened my eyes to the brutality of the workplace, my A-Level results made me vow to work hard, and the rejection letters that I still have make me appreciative of every day's work that I get.

It isn't only the positive moments of growth that help us change. You are a new person every single day, and I hope this book helps you get closer to being the person you want to be.

Damian

Thank you Geraldine for being the catalyst for positive change in our lives. Your incisive questions to make me think, your boundless patience to listen and your unwavering encouragement to take action have been invaluable from the bus stop and beyond. I love you.

George and Rose, this book – along with everything I do – is dedicated to you both. Thank you for blessing me with your all-round amazingness. I love you both.

Thank you to my amazing mum, Rosemarie, my brilliant Uncle Colin, my dear brothers, Anthony and Chris, and my sister, Rachael. Thank you to Mari and Gerry and thank you also to my nephews and nieces – Max, Jake, Ben, Joseph, Joshua, Thomas, Max and Annabel.

I owe a huge debt of gratitude to Louise Jamieson for continuing to offer your considerable talents to help me. Thank you to Teddy for your enthusiastic – and unfailingly loyal – company in all weathers. And thanks also to the unflappable David Luxton, my wonderful literary agent.

Thank you to Jake for making me think of this Luthando Daniel quote: 'A friend is someone who protects you in your absence and appreciates you in your presence.' Your quiet words of friendship, support and encouragement are invaluable and much appreciated.

Finally, this book is dedicated to the memories of my auntie, Patricia Hughes, and my dad, Brian Hughes. Your example, impact and teachings will echo throughout the generations. You may be gone but you will never be forgotten.

Jake and Damian

We would both like to thank the whole High Performance team: Hannah Smith, Finn Ryan, Will Murphy-O'Connor, Eve Hill, Demi Broughton, Jemma Smith, George Goodenough, Josh Lincoln, George MacDonald, Giac Palmiero, Chloe Dannatt, Natalie Kali, Oleg Parinov and Callum McDonnell. Your endless enthusiasm, indefatigable spirit, boundless energy and unfailing humour make a great team and an even greater impact.

We are also hugely grateful to the wider team at YMU – especially Holly Bott, Amanda Harris and Rachel Baxter.

Thank you to all our podcast guests, for investing your trust in us and sharing your incredible wisdom, insights and lessons.

Thank you also to our fantastically talented, unfailingly polite and incredibly patient editor, Rowan Borchers. Your advice, direction and guidance has been a privilege to receive. Equally, your faith, trust and support for the High Performance message is greatly appreciated. We would also like to extend our appreciation to the whole team at Penguin Random House for your passionate support of this book.

And thank you to the authors and academics whose work ignited our interest in high performance, and helped us finesse our argument. The following books had a particular impact on us during our research – they offer a good starting point for anyone looking to learn more about positive change.

Alan Deutschman's book *Change or Die* was the catalyst for this theme of transformation and his writings are always to be savoured. Dr David Rock's books were invaluable in opening up the world of neuroscience and pointing us in the necessary direction to explore the key factors behind taking the leap. Thomas Wedell-Wedellsborg's innovative and accessible work on problem-solving has been fascinating, while Rosabeth Moss Kanter's work never fails to engage. We would also suggest readers explore Chip and Dan Heath's book *Switch* as well as Richard Wiseman's extensive back catalogue.

Finally, we would like to extend our sincere thanks to you, the reader. We never lose sight of the fact that you have a dizzying amount of choice, distraction and demands upon your time and focus. Reading this far demands both. We don't take this lightly. We hope *How to Change Your Life* has been as rewarding to read as it has been to write.

NOTES

Most of the quotations in this book come from our *High Performance* podcast interviews, transcripts and recordings of which can be found at www.thehighperformancepodcast.com. These notes include only quotations and case studies from elsewhere.

Introduction: The Journey and the Map

1   Joseph Campbell, *The Hero with a Thousand Faces* (New World Library, third edition, 2012).
2   Nancy Duarte, *Illuminate: Ignite Change through Speeches, Stories, Ceremonies and Symbols* (Portfolio, 2016).

Lesson 1: What's Your Problem?

1   Mihaly Csikszentmihalyi, *Flow: The Psychology of Happiness* (Ebury, 2013).
2   J. W. Getzels and Mihaly Csikszentmihalyi, 'From problem solving to problem finding', in *Perspectives in Creativity*, ed. Irving A. Taylor and J. W. Getzels (Routledge, 2017), 90–116; J. W. Getzels, 'Problem finding: a theoretical note', *Cognitive Science*, 1979, 3(2), 167–171; J. W. Getzels, 'Problem finding and the enhancement of creativity', *NASSP Bulletin*, 1985, 69(482), 55–61.
3   This description draws upon Daniel H. Pink, *To Sell is Human: The Surprising Truth About Moving Others* (Riverhead, 2012); these findings are also summarised in James Greig, 'Are you solving the right problem?', www.greig.cc, 2016.

4   This description draws on Daniel H. Pink, *To Sell is Human: The Surprising Truth About Moving Others* (Riverhead, 2012) and James Greig, 'Are you solving the right problem?', www.greig.cc, 2016. The original research can be found at J. W. Getzels and Mihaly Csikszentmihalyi, 'From problem solving to problem finding', in *Perspectives in Creativity*, ed. Irving A. Taylor and J. W. Getzels (Routledge, 2017), 90–116; J. W. Getzels, 'Problem finding: a theoretical note', *Cognitive Science*, 1979, 3(2), 167–171; J. W. Getzels, 'Problem finding and the enhancement of creativity', *NASSP Bulletin*, 1985, 69(482), 55–61.

5   This description draws on Chip Heath and Dan Heath, *Made to Stick* (Random House, 2007). The original research is Elizabeth L. Newton (1990). 'The rocky road from actions to intentions' (PhD thesis). Stanford University. This topic was also explored in Colin Camerer, George Loewenstein and Martin Weber, 'The Curse of Knowledge in Economic Settings: An Experimental Analysis', *Journal of Political Economy,* 97 (5): 1232–1254.

6   Chip Heath and Dan Heath, *Made to Stick* (Random House, 2007). See also Chip Heath and Dan Heath, 'The curse of knowledge', *Harvard Business Review*, 2006; Chip Heath, 'Loud and Clear', *Stanford Social Innovation Review*, winter 2003.

7   Chip Heath and Dan Heath, *Made to Stick* (Random House, 2007).

8   This description is informed by Thomas Wedell-Wedellsborg, *What's Your Problem: To Solve Your Toughest Problems, Change the Problems You Solve* (Harvard Business Review Press, 2020); as well as Thomas Wedell-Wedellsborg, 'Are you solving the right problems', *Harvard Business Review*, January–February 2017, 76–83; Thomas Wedell-Wedellsborg, *Innovation as Usual: How to Help Your People Bring Great Ideas to Life* (Harvard Business Review Press, 2013).

9   Luke Rix-Standing, 'Why Alastair Campbell is opening up about his family's history of mental health struggles', *Yorkshire Post*, 29 September 2020.

10 Alastair Campbell, *Living Better: How I Learned to Survive Depression* (John Murray, 2020).

11 Alastair Campbell, *Living Better: How I Learned to Survive Depression* (John Murray, 2020); Decca Aitkenhead, 'Alastair Campbell on madness and power: "I don't mind that I'm psychologically flawed"', *Guardian*, 15 September 2017; Sally Newall, 'Could looking at your life like a jam jar improve your mental health?', *Harper's Bazaar*, 5 October 2021.

12 Alastair Campbell, *Living Better: How I Learned to Survive Depression* (John Murray, 2020).

13 Karen A. Baikie and Kay Wilhelm, 'Emotional and physical health benefits of expressive writing', *Advances in Psychiatric Treatment*, 2005, 11(5), 338–346.

14 Joshua M. Smyth, Arthur A. Stone, Adam Hurewitz and Alan Kaell, 'Effects of writing about stressful experiences on symptom reduction in patients with asthma or rheumatoid arthritis: a randomized trial', *JAMA: Journal of the American Medical Association*, 1999, 281(14), 1304–1309.

15 This account of Campbell's experiences draws upon the documentary *Alastair Campbell: Depression and Me*, BBC Two, 2019. More broadly, it draws upon a number of books and articles about Campbell, including Alastair Campbell, *Living Better: How I Learned to Survive Depression* (John Murray, 2020); Alastair Campbell, *The Blair Years* (Hutchinson, 2007); Decca Aitkenhead, 'Alastair Campbell on madness and power: "I don't mind that I'm psychologically flawed"', *Guardian*, 15 September 2017. See also Sally Newall, 'Could looking at your life like a jam jar improve your mental health?', *Harper's Bazaar*, 5 October 2021.

Lesson 2: A Better 'You'

1 The study Chatterjee described is David A. Snowdon and Nun, 'Healthy aging and dementia: findings from the Nun Study', *Annals of Internal Medicine*, 2003, 139(5 Pt 2),

450–4. More broadly, this interview drew upon a number of books and articles about Chatterjee, including his books *Feel Great Lose Weight* (Penguin Life, 2022), *Feel Better in 5* (Penguin Life, 2021) and *The Stress Solution* (Penguin Life, 2020); as well as Vicky Allan, 'Happiness. Why Rangan Chatterjee believes it makes us healthy', *Herald Scotland*, 14 May 2022 and 'How the near-death experience of his baby son utterly changed the way this doctor practises medicine,' *Belfast Telegraph*, 27 January 2018.

2   Sheldon Cohen, Cuneyt M. Alper, William J. Doyle, John J. Treanor and Ronald B. Turner, 'Positive emotional style predicts resistance to illness after experimental exposure to rhinovirus or influenza A virus', *Psychosomatic Medicine*, 2006, 68(6), 809–15.

3   Vicky Allan, 'Happiness. Why Rangan Chatterjee believes it makes us healthy', *Herald Scotland*, 14 May 2022.

4   Rangan Chatterjee, *Happy Mind, Happy Life* (Penguin Life, 2021).

5   By far most important source in writing this section was Héctor García and Francesc Miralles, *Ikigai: The Japanese Secret to a Long and Happy Life* (Hutchinson, 2017), which we highly recommend; as well as the valuable book by Ken Mogi, *The Little Book of Ikigai* (Quercus, 2019). This section also drew upon Dan Buettner's work on 'blue zones'. See Dan Buettner, *The Blue Zones: Lessons for Living Longer from the People Who've Lived the Longest* (National Geographic, 2012) and his TED Talk, 'The Blue Zones: Lessons for living longer from the people who've lived the longest'. To understand the scientific basis of *ikigai* in more detail, see Akihiro Hasegawa et al., 'Regional differences in *ikigai* (reasons for living) in elderly people: Relationship between ikigai and family structure, physiological situation and functional capacity', *Japanese Journal of Geriatrics*, 2003.

6   This exercise is inspired in part by Mogi, *The Little Book of Ikigai.*

7   This section draws upon 'Happiness', *Herald Scotland.*

8   Ibid.

9   Ibid.

10 Dean Keith Simonton, 'Talent and its development: an emergenic and epigenetic model', *Psychological Review*, 1999, 106(3), 435–457.

11 Joe Wicks, *Facing My Childhood*, BBC One. This documentary is a primary source for Cole Moreton, 'Joe Wicks: The man who moved the nation', *You Magazine*, 22 November 2020.

12 Luke Benedictus, 'Interview: How Joe Wicks stopped punching walls & learned not to yell at his kids', www.the-father-hood.com, undated.

13 Cole Moreton, 'Joe Wicks: The man who moved the nation', *You Magazine*, 22 November 2020.

14 Zoe Williams, '"My heartthrob days are over": Joe Wicks on health, happiness – and training the nation', *Guardian*, 26 March 2020.

15 This description of Barbara Fredrickson's research draws upon Chip and Dan Heath, *Switch*. The original research is Barbara L. Fredrickson, 'The role of positive emotions in positive psychology: the broaden-and-build theory of positive emotions', *American Psychologist*, 2001, 56(3), 218–26; and Barbara Fredrickson, *Positivity: Groundbreaking Research to Release Your Inner Optimist and Thrive* (Oneworld Publications, 2011).

16 Joshi Herrmann, 'Susan Ma: from poverty in Shanghai to Lord Sugar's boardroom', *Evening Standard*, 25 July 2011. This examination of what Ma's life teaches us about the 'infinite game' also draws on a conversation with Simon Sinek, who was effusive about her work.

17 Ibid.

18 Ibid.

19 This account of the 'infinite game' draws upon Simon Sinek, *The Infinite Game* (Portfolio, 2019), as well as our conversations with Sinek for the podcast.
20 Simon Sinek, *The Infinite Game* (Portfolio, 2019).
21 Ibid.

Lesson 3: The Power of Where You Are

1 Alex Scott, *How (Not) to Be Strong* (Century, 2022).
2 Ibid.
3 This account of Akers' time at Arsenal draws upon Tom Garry, 'Vic Akers: The legendary Arsenal Ladies manager who won 10 Women's FA Cups', BBC News, 12 May 2016.
4 K. Lewin, 'Environmental forces in child behavior and development', in *A Handbook of Child Psychology*, ed. C. Murchison, 94–127 (Clark University Press, 1931). This research is also featured in *Switch*, Chip and Dan Heath, which I drew upon in this portion of the text.
5 Paul Ekman, *Unmasking the Face: A Guide to Recognizing Emotions from Facial Clues* (Malor Books, 2003).
6 David Rock's writing and teachings were important resources in writing this section. His SCARF model to explain how the social brain works is accessible and inspiring. The Evian Gordon quote comes from David Rock, 'Managing with the brain in mind', www.strategy-business.com, 27 August 2007; and his books *Your Brain at Work: Strategies for Overcoming Distraction, Regaining Focus, and Working Smarter All Day Long* (Harper Business, 2020) and *Quiet Leadership: Six Steps to Transforming Performance at Work* (Harper Business, 2007) were also used in the research.
7 This account of Warrington's life primarily draws on Sarah Shephard, 'Josh Warrington, featherweight boxing champion and ... dental technician?', www.theathletic.com, 7 May 2020. Other sources include John Evans, 'Stress Management: Josh Warrington has come to terms with the

demands of his profession', *Boxing News*, 7 December 2022, and John Dennan, 'Josh Warrington: a fighter's mind, *Boxing News*, 6 December 2018.

8   Sarah Shephard, 'Josh Warrington, featherweight boxing champion and . . . dental technician?', www.theathletic.com, 7 May 2020.

9   Ibid.

10 Ibid.

11 The main source for this section is Richard Wiseman, *The Luck Factor* (Century, 2003). The original studies it cites are V. H. Medvec, S. F. Madey and T. Gilovich T, 'When less is more: counterfactual thinking and satisfaction among Olympic medalists', *Journal of Personality and Social Psychology*, 1995, 69(4), 603–10; D. Matsumoto and B. Willingham, 'The thrill of victory and the agony of defeat: spontaneous expressions of medal winners of the 2004 Athens Olympic Games', *Journal of Personality and Social Psychology*, 2006, 91(3), 568–81; and Jason G. Goldman, 'Why bronze medalists are happier than silver winners', *Scientific American*, 9 August 2012.

12 Richard Wiseman, *The Luck Factor: Change Your Luck and Change Your Life* (Century, 2003).

13 This pitstop draws upon Mercedes Aranda et al., 'Relationship between organizational socialization and attitudes and behaviours in volunteers: the importance of organizational justice', *Revista de Psicología Social*, 2018.

14 The main source for this account of Thorpe's life is Michael Cowley, 'A career that sets the gold standard', *Sydney Morning Herald*, 22 November 2006. Additional sources include 'Up, up and away', *Sydney Morning Herald*, 2 July 2022; Gary Smith, 'The man with the golden feet', *Sports Illustrated*, 22 November 1999; and Paul Mason, 'Heroes of swimming: Ian Thorpe', *Guardian*, 15 April 2014. See also Ian Thorpe, *This Is Me: The Autobiography* (Simon & Schuster, 1998).

15 Michael Cowley, 'A career that sets the gold standard', *Sydney Morning Herald*, 22 November 2006.

16 Steven F. Maier et al., 'Behavioral control, the medial prefrontal cortex, and resilience', *Dialogues in Clinical Neuroscience*, 2006, 8(4), 397–406.

17 E. J. Langer and J. Rodin, 'The effects of choice and enhanced personal responsibility for the aged: A field experiment in an institutional setting', *Journal of Personality and Social Psychology, 34* (2)191–198, 1976. For a wider exploration of the relationship between autonomy, control and mood, see H. M. Lefcourt et al., 'Locus of control as a modifier of the relationship between stressors and moods,' *Journal of Personality and Social Psychology, 41*(2), 357–369.

18 Quoted in Gary Smith, 'Ian Thorpe finds inspiration from a brave young friend', *Sports Illustrated*, 22 November 1999.

Lesson 4: The Power of Who You're With

1 This quote comes from Liz Byrnes, 'Mel Marshall on some dark days and her message to Peaty after Rio glory', swimmingworldmagazine.com, 14 July 2021. More broadly, this account of Marshall's life draws on various conversations with Damian over the years, as well as an excellent keynote speech she delivered at UK Sport in 2016, which Damian attended. Other articles used in the research of this relationship were: Craig Lord, 'Why Mel Marshall Tops Swimming World's International Coach of the Year Chart', swimmingworldmagazine.com, 28 December 2019; and Adam Peaty's book, *The Gladiator Mindset: Push Your Limits. Overcome Challenges. Achieve Your Goals* (Quercus, 2021).

2 Liz Byrnes, 'Mel Marshall on some dark days and her message to Peaty after Rio glory', swimmingworldmagazine.com, 14 July 2021.

3 Ibid.

4 Ibid.

5   Naomi I. Eisenberger, 'Broken hearts and broken bones: a neural perspective on the similarities between social and physical pain', *Current Directions in Psychological Science*, 2012, 21(1), 42–47; Naomi I. Eisenberger, Matthew D. Lieberman and Kipling D Williams, 'Does rejection hurt? An fMRI study of social exclusion', *Science*, 2003, 302(5643), 290–92.

6   Ibid.

7   Vicky Pattison, *The Secret to Happy: How to Build Resilience, Banish Self-doubt and Live the Life You Deserve* (Sphere, 2022).

8   Judith Woods, 'Vicky Pattison: "Reality TV made my life . . . and ruined it"', *Daily Mail*, 21 March 2021.

9   Ibid.

10   Quote from O. Brafman and R. Brafman, *Sway: The Irresistible Pull of Irrational Behavior* (Doubleday, 2007). The original research can be found in David Kantor, *Reading the Room: Group Dynamics for Coaches and Leaders* (Wiley, 2012); David Kantor and Lehr William, *Inside the Family* (Meredith Winter, 2003) as well as David Kantor, 'The Family's Construction of Reality', *Family Process*, 21 (4):483–485 (1982). This research is also discussed in Peter Senge, *The Fifth Discipline* (Century Business, 1990) and Bill Isaacs, *Dialogue and the Art of Thinking Together* (Bantam, 1999).

11   Brafman and Brafman, *Sway*.

12   This pitstop draws upon Kantor, *Reading the Room*.

13   Moira Petty, 'Adventurer Bear Grylls' battle with back pain and high cholesterol', *Daily Mail*, 24 April 2007.

14   Stuart Jeffries, 'Bear Grylls: "There's no point getting to the summit if you're an arsehole"', *Guardian*, 16 February 2021. This exploration of Grylls' psychology also drew upon his own books *Never Give Up: A Life of Adventure* (Bantam Press, 2022) and *Mud, Sweat and Tears* (Bantam Press, 2022).

15   Stuart Jeffries, 'Bear Grylls: "You don't need muscles or good looks"', *Irish Times*, 19 February 2021.

16 Thomas Brenner and Nichola J. Vriend, 'On the behaviour of proposers in ultimatum games', *Journal of Economic Behavior & Organization*, 2006, 61 (4): 617–631.

17 Golnaz Tabibnia, Ajay B. Satpute and Matthew D. Lieberman, 'The sunny side of fairness: preference for fairness activates reward circuitry (and disregarding unfairness activates self-control circuitry', *Psychological Science*, 2008, 19(4), 339–347. I first came across this research in David Rock, op. cit.

18 Stuart Jeffries, 'Bear Grylls: "There's no point getting to the summit if you're an arsehole"', *Guardian*, 16 February 2021.

Lesson 5: The Obstacles to Change

1 This account of Fury's life draws upon our interview as well as his books, including *Behind the Mask* (Century, 2022) and *The Furious Method* (Century, 2021). I also drew upon the accounts of his life in Bruce Thomas, *Tyson Fury: Fighting Shadows* (independently published, 2019) and Paris Fury, *Love and Fury* (Hodder, 2022).

2 Martin Domin, 'Tyson Fury reveals he drove Ferrari towards bridge at 190mph in suicide attempt', *Daily Mirror*, 26 October 2018; the quote itself originated in *The Joe Rogan Podcast*, although Fury also recounted this story on *High Performance*. See also Tyson Fury *Gloves Off* (Century, 2022), which recounts this story in more detail.

3 Brené Brown, 'Brené on Day 2', *Unlocking Us with Brené Brown* podcast, brenebrown.com, 2 September 2020. Brown's work has been a important source. Her books *Daring Greatly: How the Courage to Be Vulnerable Transforms the Way We Live, Love, Parent, and Lead* and *Atlas of the Heart: Mapping Meaningful Connection and the Language of Human Experience* are worth including as references.

4 Rosabeth Moss Kanter, 'Change is hardest in the middle', *Harvard Business Review*, 12 August 2009. This section also draws upon Rosabeth Moss Kanter, *Evolve! Succeeding*

in the Digital Culture of Tomorrow (Harvard Business School Press, 2001) and Rosabeth Moss Kanter, *Leadership for Change: Enduring Skills for Change Masters* (Harvard Business School Press, 2020).

5   Dr Pippa Grange, *Fear Less: How to Win at Life Without Losing Yourself* (Vermilion, 2020).

6   This quote comes from Grange's 2020 interview, 'When Fear Shows Up: Our Expert Interview With Pippa Grange' (mindtools.com, 24 December 2020). See also Pippa Grange, *Fear Less: How to Win at Life Without Losing Yourself* (Vermilion, 2020).

7   Ibid.

8   Dominic Fifield, 'England team "have created their own history", says Gareth Southgate', *Guardian*, 4 July 2018.

9   Emine Saner, 'How the psychology of the England football team could change your life', *Guardian*, 10 July 2018.

10   Fifield, op cit.

11   Simon Mundie, 'Leadership: Eddie Jones', *Life Lessons: From Sport and Beyond* podcast, November 2021.

12   Simon Mundie, 'Observant Eddie Jones feels at home being England's outsider', *Guardian*, 1 November 2021.

13   Eddie Jones, *My Life and Rugby* (Macmillan, 2019).

14   Donald McRae, 'James Haskell: Eddie Jones is like a nuclear bomb waiting to go off', *Guardian*, 18 April 2016. I also used this article in the research: Johnny Watterson, 'Eddie Jones continues to revel in putting rugby's nose out of joint', *The Irish Times*, 17 February 2020.

15   Press Association, 'England's James Haskell: "Eddie Jones knows how to get the best out of me"', *Guardian*, 12 June 2016; Donald McRae, 'James Haskell: Eddie Jones is like a nuclear bomb waiting to go off'; Paul Rees, 'James Haskell: 'There are players all around with demons in their heads"', *Guardian*, 1 October 2020.

16   Simon Mundie, 'Observant Eddie Jones feels at home being England's outsider', *Guardian*, 1 November 2021.

17 G. Loewenstein, 'The psychology of curiosity: a review and reinterpretation', *Psychological Bulletin*, 1994, 116(1), 75–98; Daniel Gilbert, *Stumbling on Happiness* (Knopf, 2006); Celeste Kidd and Benjamin Y. Hayden, 'The psychology and neuroscience of curiosity', *Neuron*, 2015, 88(3), 449–460.

18 Jonah Lehrer, 'The itch of curiosity', *Wired*, 3 August 2010; Todd B. Kashdan, David J. Disabato, Fallon R. Goodman and Carl Naughton, 'The five dimensions of curiosity', *Harvard Business Review*, September–October 2018.

19 Andy Hunter, 'Jürgen Klopp can turn doubt into belief with Liverpool Capital One Cup victory', *Guardian*, 26 February 2016.

20 Jordan Henderson, *The Autobiography* (Michael Joseph, 2022).

21 Donald McRae, 'Jordan Henderson, "I was in a very dark place. It made me a lot stronger"', *Guardian*, 1 January 2021.

22 Chris Hoy introduced us to the Father Christmas Question on the *High Performance* podcast. The ideas in this section draw heavily on Hoy's mentor, Steve Peters, and particularly his remarkable book *The Chimp Paradox* (Vermilion, 2012), which we recommend very highly.

Lesson 6: Reframe Setbacks

1 This quote is from Donald McRae, 'Rob Burrow: "I've had such a wonderful life. I want to make the most of the time I have left"', *Guardian*, 7 May 2021. More broadly, this account of the Burrows' life together is informed by Rob's astonishing autobiography, *Too Many Reasons to Live* (Macmillan, 2021).

2 Ibid.

3 Ibid.

4 Ximena B. Arriaga and Caryl E. Rusbult, 'Standing in my partner's shoes: partner perspective taking and reactions to accommodative dilemmas', *Personality and Social*

Psychology Bulletin, 1998, 24(9), 927–948; Igor Grossmann and Ethan Kross, 'Exploring Solomon's paradox: self-distancing eliminates the self-other asymmetry in wise reasoning about close relationships in younger and older adults', *Psychological Science*, 2014, 25(8), 1571–1580.

5   Ozlem Ayduk and Ethan Kross, 'From a distance: implications of spontaneous self-distancing for adaptive self-reflection', *Journal of Personality and Social Psychology*, 2010, 98(5), 809–829. This section also drew upon Keith Stanovich, 'The cognitive miser: ways to avoid thinking', from *What Intelligence Tests Miss* (Yale University Press, 2011). With thanks to Rangan Chatterjee for putting us onto Kross' research, which is what ultimately led us to Igor Grossman's work on 'Solomon's Paradox'.

6   Renee Jain, 'The way you talk to your kids and yourself matters', HuffPost, updated 29 May 2016.

7   Mark Hedley, '"People couldn't imagine it being done." Nims Purja makes the impossible routine', Square Mile, 31 August 2020.

8   Ben Morse and Celine Ramseyer, 'As he scaled world's 14 highest peaks, Nepalese climber shocked by climate change effects', CNN, 6 December 2019.

9   Dominic Bliss, 'The Nepalese Mountaineer Taking a Spiritual View to New Heights', *National Geographic*, 21 January 2021,

10 Nimsdai Purja, *Beyond Possible: One Soldier, Fourteen Peaks – My Life in the Death Zone* (Hodder & Stoughton, 2020).

11 Daniel Kahneman, *Thinking, Fast and Slow* (Penguin, 2011).

12 Matthew McConaughey, *Greenlights* (Headline, 2020).

13 Rachel Syme, 'The McConaissance', *New Yorker*, 16 January 2014.

14 Ibid.

15 This description of solutions-focused therapy draws upon Chip and Dan Heath, *Switch* (2010) and to a lesser extent

Linda Metcalf, *The Miracle Question: Answer It and Change Your Life* (2006). The original research can be found at Steve de Shazer, *Keys to Solution in Brief Therapy* (Norton, 1985).

16 Ibid.

17 W. J. Gingerich and L. T. Peterson, 'Effectiveness of solution-focused brief therapy: a systematic qualitative review of controlled outcome studies', *Database of Abstracts of Reviews of Effects*, 2013.

18 Rachel Syme, 'The McConaissance'.

19 Ibid.

Lesson 7: From Actions to Systems

1 This account of Ian McGeechan's career draws upon his autobiography, *Lion Man: The Autobiography* (Simon & Schuster, 2010) and Tom English, *The Grudge: Two Nations, One Match, No Holds Barred* (Random House, 2011).

2 This account of Ash Dykes' adventures draws upon Helen Coffey, 'Ash Dykes: Meet the self-taught British adventurer who's taking on the Yangtze River', 7 March 2018; as well as Joe Ellison, '5 near-death experiences and what one adventurer learned from them', redbull.com, 20 August 2018.

3 Teresa Amabile and Steven Kramer, *The Progress Principle*, *Harvard Business Review*, 2011.

4 This account of Ben Francis' life was informed by an article by Ben Machell, 'How Ben Francis built the billion-pound fitness brand Gymshark', *The Times*, 5 December 2020.

5 This case study appears in Marshall Goldsmith, *Triggers* (Profile Books, 2015). See also Thomas Goetz, 'Harnessing the power of feedback loops', *Wired*, 19 June 2011.

6 The first five stages here are informed by the study of grief; see Elizabeth Kubler-Ross and David Kessler, *On Grief and Grieving* (Simon and Schuster, 2014).

7 Dr Ceri Evans, *Perform Under Pressure: Change the Way You Feel, Think and Act Under Pressure* (Thorsons, 2019).

We were first made aware of the 'red zone' concept by New Zealand rugby legend Dan Carter, who worked with Evans for the All Blacks.

8   This case study draws on Malcolm Gladwell, *The Tipping Point: How Little Things Can Make a Big Difference* (Little, Brown, 2000), as well as Sam Thomas Davies, 'This study reveals the tipping point in behaviour change (and how you can use it), www.samuelthomasdavies.com, 29 May 2023. The original study can be found at Howard Leventhal, 'Effects of fear and specificity of recommendation upon attitudes and behavior', *Journal of Personality and Social Psychology*, 1965, 2(1), 20–29.

9   For more information on her method see Roxie Nafousi, *Manifest* (Michael Joseph, 2022).

Lesson 8: The Final Straight

1   This description of the X-spot draws upon Shawn Achor, *Before Happiness: Five Actionable Strategies to Create a Positive Path to Success* (Virgin Books, 2013). See also Jane E. Allen, 'Adrenaline-fueled sprint makes some marathons deadly', ABC News, 21 November 2011.

2   Kate Hutchinson, 'AJ Tracey: "I had to do everything on my own"', *Guardian*, 27 October 2019.

3   Ibid.

4   Christian Jarrett, 'How to make deadlines motivating, not stressful', BBC Worklife, 10 April 2020. For a broader exploration of this phenomenon see A. Emanuel et al., 'Why do people increase effort near a deadline? An opportunity-cost model of goal gradients', *Journal of Experimental Psychology*, 2022.

5   Kelly Holmes, *Black, White & Gold: My Autobiography* (Virgin Books, 2008).

6   This exploration of Robbins' work draws upon her books, including *The 5 Second Rule* (Post Hill Press, 2017) and *The High 5 Habit* (Hay House, 2023).

7   Gretchen Rubin, 'Mel Robbins: Author Interview', gretchen-rubin.com, 1 September 2021.

8   Michael W. Kraus, Cassey Huang and Dacher Keltner, 'Tactile communication, cooperation, and performance: an ethological study of the NBA', *Emotion*, 2010, 10(5), 745–749; described in Stephanie Pappas, 'Touchy-feely NBA teams more likely to win', NBC News, 12 November 2010.

9   Mel Robbins, *The High 5 Habit: Take Control of Your Life With One Simple Habit* (Hay House, 2021).

10   This description of Konta's life draws upon our interview with her and also Jan Moir, 'Johanna Konta once made her big sister cry during Monopoly', *Daily Mail*, 12 July 2017.

Lesson 9: Your Next Adventure

1   Harry Redknapp, *Always Managing: My Autobiography* (Ebury, 2013). I also used *Behind Closed Doors: Life, Laughs and Football* (2019) by Gary Lineker and Danny Baker and *Born to Manage* by Terry Venables as research books for this section.

2   Peter E. Doolittle, 'Understanding cooperative learning through Vygotsky's zone of proximal development' (Lilly National Conference on Excellence in College Teaching, Columbia, South Carolina, 2–4 June 1995); Cathrine Hasse, 'Institutional creativity: the relational zone of proximal development', *Culture & Psychology*, 2001, 7(2), 199–221; Saul McLeod, 'Vygotsky's zone of proximal development and scaffolding', Simply Psychology, 14 May 2023.

3   Daniel Coyle, *The Talent Code: Greatness Isn't Born. It's Grown* (Arrow, 2010).

4   James Kettler, 'Essex-born stand-up Russell Kane heads to Yorkshire with new comedy tour', *Yorkshire Post*, 3 May 2019.

5   Ibid.

6 Russell Kane, *Son of a Silverback: Growing Up in the Shadow of an Alpha Male* (Bantam Press, 2019); Brian Logan, 'Russell Kane: "What am I going to do when I'm not the next big thing?"', *Guardian*, 18 September 2011.

7 James Kettler, 'Essex-born stand-up Russell Kane heads to Yorkshire with new comedy tour', *Yorkshire Post*, 3 May 2019.

8 Dave Allan, Matt Kingdon, Kris Murrin, Daz Rudkin, *What If? How to Start a Creative Revolution at Work* (Capstone, 2001).

Lesson 10: Pass It On

1 John McAvoy and Mark Turley, *Redemption: From Iron Bars to Ironman* (Pitch, 2016).

2 Niamh Lewis, 'John McAvoy: The ex-armed robber who reformed through sport in high security prison', BBC Sport, 22 October 2020.

3 Alan Deutschman, *Change or Die: The Three Keys to Change at Work and in Life* (Harper Business, 2007) and Alan Deutschman, *Walk the Walk* (Penguin, 2011).

4 Niamh Lewis, 'John McAvoy: The ex-armed robber who reformed through sport in high security prison', BBC Sport, 22 October 2020.

5 Ibid.

6 Ibid.

7 Alan Deutschman, *Change or Die*.

8 The original research is summarised in John Bowlby, *A Secure Base* (Routledge, 2005). For a more accessible introduction to attachment theory see Amir Levine and Rachel Heller, *Attached* (Bluebird, 2019).

9 John McAvoy and Mark Turley, *Redemption: From Iron Bars to Ironman* (Pitch, 2016).

10 John M. Gottman and Nan Silver, *The Seven Principles for Making Marriage Work: A Practical Guide from the*

Country's Foremost Relationship Expert (Harmony, 2015). See also John Gottman, *The Relationship Cure: A Five-Step Guide for Building Better Connections With Family, Friends, And Lovers* (Crown, 2001).

11 Sebastian Bailey and Octavius Black, *Mind Gym: Achieve More by Thinking Differently* (HarperOne, 2014)

12 John McAvoy and Mark Turley, *Redemption: From Iron Bars to Ironman* (Pitch, 2016).

13 Ibid.

14 Alan Deutschman, *Change or Die.*

15 Niamh Lewis, 'John McAvoy: The ex-armed robber who reformed through sport in high security prison', BBC Sport, 22 October 2020.

16 John McAvoy and Mark Turley, *Redemption: From Iron Bars to Ironman* (Pitch, 2016).

17 Ibid.

18 Niamh Lewis, 'John McAvoy: The ex-armed robber who reformed through sport in high security prison', BBC Sport, 22 October 2020.

19 Alan Deutschman, *Change or Die.*

20 Niamh Lewis, 'John McAvoy: The ex-armed robber who reformed through sport in high security prison', BBC Sport, 22 October 2020.

21 Ibid.

Conclusion: The Never-ending Journey

1 Frances Bridges, 'Anthony Bourdain's most poignant reflections on life and travel', *Forbes*, 11 June 2018.

INDEX

ABOUT THE AUTHORS

Jake Humphrey is one of Britain's best-respected sports presenters. Formerly lead Premier League presenter at BT Sport, Jake has covered events ranging from Formula 1 to the London Olympics and was the youngest ever presenter of the BBC's *Match of the Day*.

Damian Hughes is an expert on high-performing cultures. A trusted advisor to businesses and sportspeople around the world, he has been praised by the likes of Richard Branson, Muhammad Ali, Roger Bannister and Alex Ferguson.

Jake and Damian are the creators of **High Performance**, the UK's most-downloaded podcast on the psychology of success. In its first three years, they have interviewed unicorn-founding CEOs and World Heavyweight Champion boxers, completed two sell-out tours, and published the huge *Sunday Times* best-seller *High Performance*.

CONTINUE YOUR
HIGH PERFORMANCE JOURNEY

Also available from Jake Humphrey and Damian Hughes . . .

Read *High Performance: Lessons from the Best on Becoming Your Best*

Complete *High Performance: The Daily Journal*

Listen to the *High Performance* podcast

Watch the *High Performance* YouTube series

Learn about the *High Performance* foundation

Join the *High Performance* members club